"I now own *24-Carat Commercials for Kids* and *Magnificent Monologues for Kids* and I am one happy acting teacher! When I started teaching children, I realized that good contemporary material for students is hard to come by. I made a few purchases...*Magnificent Monologues for Kids* was one of them. Needless to say, the kids waited in line to use this book to select a monologue rather than the others I had purchased. When I received the commercial book, I knew within 10 minutes that it was a winner. Chambers is making my job as a teacher easier and much more fun!"

—JAN HARLYE-SOULE, DRAMA TEACHER
ALEMEDA, CA

"As Nickelodeon and Disney emerge as major networks, the market for teen and pre-teen actors for TV, movies, theater and commercials is in a boom phase. Stevens helps youngsters go after these jobs. He has worked with actors ranging from high-profile performers to countless youngsters getting steady work in commercials."

—MIKE HOLTZCLAW, THE DAILY PRESS
VIRGINIA BEACH, VA

"Chambers Stevens is a talented actor and teacher. I learned so much about the acting business. He taught me not only how I could succeed in acting but how I should follow my dreams even if they weren't about show business. Chambers, you da man!"

—ANNIE MCGHEE, STUDENT ACTRESS
CHARLESTON CATHOLIC HIGH SCHOOL

"Chambers Stevens conducted a fantastic workshop. He clearly knows his craft and more importantly knows how to and enjoys working with kids."

—DAVID HOUGH, COMMUNITY RELATIONS COORDINATOR
BORDERS BOOKS & MUSIC, CHESTNUT HILL, MA

Sensational Scenes for Teens!

What Others Are Saying About the Hollywood 101 series

"Chambers is so cool! He taught me a lot and encouraged me to pursue my dreams! He understands kids and teenagers better than any adult I've ever met."

—ASHLEY LATON, STUDENT ACTOR
HURRICANE HIGH SCHOOL

"Chambers writes {characters that are} sometimes moving, often funny and always entertaining. Chambers is a superb actor, willing to take risks in pursuit of his goals, stretching our imagination to his creative limit as he perfects his craft."

—JEFF ELLIS, EDITOR, SOME MAGAZINE

"I've seen students transform under Chambers' guidance. He inspires them to do their best."

—APRIL MARTIN, WEST VIRGINIA STATE COLLEGE, WV

"I always see the genuine trust that kids have for Chambers. It allows them to be free in their craft."

—SCOTT DUNCAN, VP, TRILLION PICTURES

"Chambers and his books are great! He draws out the best from the kids."

—MICHAEL ZODOROZNY, ANIMATOR
DOUG, DARIA, BEAVIS AND BUTTHEAD

Hollywood 101's *Magnificent Monologues for Kids* "will fill a gap in library collections, whether as a source for auditioning materials or for short oral presentations."

—BOOKLIST, AMERICAN LIBRARY ASSOCIATION

"Chambers captures the language of youth!"

—CHARLOTTE ANGEL, PRODUCER, PRIME

The Scene Studyguide for Teen Actors!

Hollywood 101

SENSATIONAL SCENES for teens

"The Scene Studyguide
for Teen Actors!"

by

Chambers Stevens

SANDCASTLE
PUBLISHING &
DISTRIBUTION
south pasadena, california

Sensational Scenes for Teens: The Scene Studyguide for Teen Actors!
Copyright © 2001 by Chambers Stevens
Book Cover & Interior Design by Renee Rolle-Whatley
Book Cover Photography by Karl Preston
The images used herein were obtained from IMSI's Master Clips©/MasterPhotos© Collection, 1895
Francisco Blvd. East, San Rafael, CA 94901-5506, USA

Actors in Cover Photograph: Leanna Boyer, Laila Dagher, Abigail McFarlane, Lisa Michelle, Edwin Martel
Hodge, Nate Campbell, Rahi Azizi, Michael Allen Moreno, Alexander Collins, Mark Allan Stauback

Published by: Sandcastle Publishing & Distribution

Post Office Box 3070
South Pasadena, CA 91031-6070
Phone/FAX/email (323) 255-3616, info@sandcastle-online.com

This publication is designed to reflect accurate and authoritative information with regard to the subject covered at the time of publication. It is sold as is, without warranty of any kind, either express or implied,
respecting the contents of this book, including but not limited to implied warranties for the book's quality,
performance, merchantability, or fitness for any particular purpose. The author and publisher assume no
responsibility for errors, inaccuracies, omissions or any other inconsistency herein. Neither the author, publisher or its dealers or distributors shall be liable to the purchaser or any other person or entity with respect
to any liability, loss, or damage caused or alleged to be cased directly or indirectly by this book. It is sold
with the understanding that the book provides educational material and is not rendering other professional
recommendations. Any slights against people or organizations are unintentional.

Publisher's Cataloging in Publication
(Provided by Quality Books, Inc.)

Stevens, Chambers.
    Sensational scenes for teens : "the scene studyguide
for teen actors!" / Chambers Stevens,
Renee Rolle-Whatley. -- 1st ed.
    p. cm. -- (Hollywood 101 ; 3)
    Includes bibliographical references and index.
    LCCN: 99-76948
    ISBN: 1-883995-10-8

    1. Acting. 2. Teenagers--Drama. 3. Young
adult drama. 4. Acting--Auditions
I. Rolle-Whatley, Renee. II. Title. III. Series.

PN2080.S74 2000   812.6
                      QBI00-513

First Printing 2/01

Printed and bound in the United States of America
06 05 04 03 02 01   10 9 8 7 6 5 4 3 2

Table of Contents

Dedication

TO

MY DIRECTING TEACHER

MARITA WOODRUFF

&

MY WRITING TEACHER

RETA MADSEN

MAY THIS BOOK INSPIRE OTHERS

THE SAME WAY YOU INSPIRED ME

For the last ten years, I've been an acting coach in Los Angeles. The kids I've coached have worked on Broadway, in major motion pictures and in television: on ABC, NBC, CBS, FOX, WB, UPN, The Disney Channel and Nickelodeon. They've also done voice-overs for cartoons and video games. Recently, two kids that I coach booked shows on the internet. It's an exciting time to be a young actor.

How do these kids get all these jobs? Well, I would like to think that it's because they have a good coach. But the truth is—they practice. While many kids in America are watching TV, playing outside or practicing piano, many young actors are practicing their craft of acting. They take classes, learn lines and go to auditions. If you want to be a great guitar player, you have to practice. It's the same for acting. I hope this book will help you exercise your talent.

This is my third book in the series Hollywood 101. The first book, **MAGNIFICENT MONOLOGUES FOR KIDS: EVERYTHING KIDS NEED TO KNOW TO GET THE PART,** was written to help young actors learn to audition. Most theatrical play auditions and theatrical agents require a memorized monologue. My second book, **24-CARAT COMMERCIALS FOR KIDS: EVERYTHING KIDS NEED TO KNOW TO BREAK INTO COMMERCIALS**, was obviously written to help kids learn how to get commercial jobs.

 **Introduction**

After these first two books came out, I received lots of mail from young actors, directors and teachers asking me for a scene book for teenagers. I soon found out why. While doing research for this book, I realized that most scene books on the market for teens were written by people who seemed to get their ideas from 1950s TV shows. The characters say lines like, *"Jeez Dad, why can't I take the jalopy to the malt shop?"*

In **SENSATIONAL SCENES FOR TEENS: THE SCENE STUDYGUIDE FOR TEEN ACTORS!** you will find scenes that could be on today's TV shows. Some are written in the style of half-hour sitcoms (situation comedies). Others are written in the style of hour long dramas. I've also included a number of exercises you can work on while performing the scenes. The glossary has been expanded and I've included a bibliography on plays I think you should read. They're written by some of the greatest writers in the world. And as any actor will tell you, *"It's impossible to give a great performance in a bad play."* So check them out. You'll be surprised at what you'll learn.

Good luck. And most importantly, have fun.

There are two different kinds of scenes in this book:

• Half-hour comedy scenes

• One-hour drama scenes

Half-hour comedy scripts, like *Friends, Kenan & Kel, The Brady Bunch* and *Mary Tyler Moore* look like this:

<u>INT. THE SCIENCE LAB</u>

HOWIE IS WORKING ON A SCIENCE EXPERIMENT WHEN DANNY ENTERS.

DANNY
Hey Howie! How's it going?

HOWIE
Danny, I haven't seen you in a while.

Notice that the stage direction, the line that starts HOWIE IS—, is typed in capital letters. Also notice that the slugline, that's the line that tells us where the scene takes place, is underlined. By the way, INT. stands for interior and means inside. EXT. stands for Exterior and means outside.

Scene Styles

One-hour drama scripts like *Buffy the Vampire Slayer*, *Party of Five* and *Little House on the Prairie* look like this:

EXT. A STREET

Leanna and Stephanie are walking home.

> **LEANNA**
> I'm not lying for you.

> **STEPHANIE**
> Come on.

Notice the slugline is not underlined. Also, the stage directions are in lower and uppercase letters.

Okay you say, I understand the difference. Now, what good does it do me? Well, plenty.

Half-hour comedy shows are taped before a live audience. An actor performing in a half-hour show must understand that as in a play, he/she must hold for laughs. There are usually three cameras and the actors rehearse for a couple of days before taping. The actual taping usually lasts about four hours.

Hour-long shows are filmed with one camera. There is no audience and usually no rehearsal. Filming an hour drama can take as long as 7 to 8 days.

There are of course exceptions, but in Hollywood, that's usually the case.

Sensational Scenes for Teens!

Cast Me

<u>INT. THE DRAMA ROOM</u>

THE CAST LIST FOR THE NEW PLAY IS TAPED TO THE WALL.
STACEY AND TERESA RUN IN.

> STACEY
> (Running toward the list) It's up! It's up!

> TERESA
> (Pulling her back) Wait! Don't look yet!

> STACEY
> Why?

> TERESA
> What if we're not on it?

> STACEY
> (Going toward the list) We'll be on it.

> TERESA
> (Pulling her back) But what if we don't get the leads?

> STACEY
> Could that happen?

> TERESA
> It could happen.

> STACEY
> You mean we'd be like—in...?

> TERESA
> (Nodding her head) Supporting roles!

> STACEY
> That's horrible!

> TERESA
> Or worse. We could be in the—

> STACEY
> Don't say it.

> TERESA
> Chorus!

> STACEY
> (Starting to cry) Stop! Stop! That's disgusting!

TERESA
Calm down. It's okay. We're not in the chorus yet.

STACEY
What if we don't even make the show? What if we have to work on the crew or something?

BOTH
Ahh!!!!!!!!

TERESA
(Now crying) I'm not building the sets. Last time I nailed my hand to the floor. I still have the scar.

STACEY
We'll, I'm not doing wardrobe. Remember when we did You're A Good Man Charlie Brown and I had to stay after school to clean the dog costume?

TERESA
Gross.

STACEY
Look, lets make a deal. No matter what, we're not going to be on the crew.

TERESA
(Shaking hands) Right. And we won't be in the chorus either.

STACEY
Yeah!

TERESA
In fact if Mr. Grant can't appreciate our talent, we won't even be in the show at all!

STACEY
We're too cool to be in the play anyway.

TERESA
Let's get out of here. Who wants to be in the stupid play anyway?

THEY EXIT. A BEAT. THEY RUN BACK ON.

BOTH
(Looking at the list) Ah!!!!!!!!!!!

BMOC

INT. THE SCIENCE LAB

HOWIE IS WORKING ON A SCIENCE EXPERIMENT WHEN DANNY
ENTERS. (NOTE: DANNY AND HOWIE ARE KIND OF NERDY.)

> DANNY
> Hey, Howie! How's it going?

> HOWIE
> Danny, I haven't seen you in a while.

> DANNY
> Well, my girlfriend has been keeping me busy.

> HOWIE
> (Shocked) Girlfriend? You're kidding right?

> DANNY
> No, I'm dating Stacey Scott.

HOWIE STARTS LAUGHING HYSTERICALLY.

> HOWIE
> Stacey Scott? The homecoming queen? That's a good one.

> DANNY
> I am dating her. (Taking out his wallet) See, this is me and
> Stacey at the fall dance.

> HOWIE
> (Looking at the picture) This is good. Did you make this on
> your computer?

> DANNY
> (Starting to get angry) No! This is real.

HOWIE STOPS LAUGHING.

> HOWIE
> Wow! How did you do it?

> DANNY
> Well, I asked her out and she said yes.

HOWIE
Not that. I mean how did you do it?

DANNY
Do what?

HOWIE
Transform yourself from a huge nerd to the BMOC.

DANNY
BMOC?

HOWIE
Big man on campus.

DANNY
I was never a nerd!

HOWIE
Oh, come on! You're like me. We're nerds, geeks, wimps. Don't look so surprised. You know it's true.

DANNY
I had no idea you thought of me that way.

HOWIE
Everybody thinks of you that way. Heck everybody thinks of me that way.

DANNY
(Insulted) Thanks a lot.

HOWIE
But look at you now. You're cool. Hip. You're the man. How did you do it?

DANNY
I didn't do anything.

HOWIE
Come on.

DANNY
(Whispering) All right. All right. I wasn't going to tell anybody but you're my friend so...

HOWIE
Tell me!

DANNY
Well, Howie you know me and you are scientists. Kind of. I mean someday we will be.

HOWIE
Right.

DANNY
So as a scientist, I looked at the facts. And the facts said, I was a loser.

HOWIE
I wouldn't be that harsh.

DANNY
It's true. When it came to getting a girlfriend, I didn't have a chance in...well you know what. So I started studying girls. Like any good scientist, I wanted to learn about their behavior, their likes and dislikes. And after a couple of months of this, I came up with a plan.

HOWIE
Oh, this is good.

DANNY
You see, the girls I studied all had one thing in common. They liked guys who listened to them.

HOWIE
That's it?

DANNY
No, I mean really listened. You know, cared about what they thought. In my experiments, I learned that most guys go on dates and talk only about themselves. Girls hate that.

HOWIE
Makes sense.

DANNY
So I walked up to Stacey and asked her how she was doing. Well, she looked at me kind of funny and started to walk off. I just stood there. She got half way down the hall and then looked back. She saw me standing there waiting for her answer. So she walked back. And said, "You really want to know?" I said, "Yes." And she told me. It had been a bad day for her. Big test. She hurt her ankle in cheer-leading practice. Her mother got arrested for shoplifting. Anyway, I just stood there and listened. Didn't say a word. Didn't offer advice, try to change the subject, no, I just lis-tened. We've been dating ever since.

HOWIE
(Starting to cry) That's the most moving story I've ever heard.

DANNY
Yeah, well, it worked for me. So Howie now it's your turn. Find the girl of your dreams. Walk up to her and—LISTEN.

Detention

<u>INT. THE DETENTION ROOM</u>

EMILY AND BETSY ARE SITTING IN DETENTION.

> BETSY
> So what are you in for?

> EMILY
> Chewing gum. You?

> BETSY
> Passing notes.

> EMILY
> Bummer.

> BETSY
> Yeah, major bummer.

> EMILY
> So, what do we do in here?

> BETSY
> You've never had detention before?

> EMILY
> Nope. This is my first time.

> BETSY
> We do nothing. We just sit here for an hour.

> EMILY
> That's easy.

> BETSY
> It's harder than it looks.

A BEAT.

> EMILY
> Hey, you got any gum?

> BETSY
> (Looking through her purse) I might—

EMILY
(Starting to shake) Good, I really need a piece.

BETSY
Look at you. You're shaking.

EMILY
I love gum. I need gum! PLEASE HAVE SOME GUM!!!

BETSY
Girl, you're addicted aren't you?

EMILY
No, I can live without it.

BETSY
Yeah, I bet. (Finding a piece of gum in her purse) Then I
guess you won't be needing this!

EMILY
(Reaching for the gum) Please give it to me. Please! Please!
Pleeeeese!!!!

BETSY
Okay! Okay! (Handing her the gum) You're sad. No wonder you got detention.

EMILY AND BETSY SIT THERE FOR A BEAT. THEN EMILY PULLS
OUT A PIECE OF PAPER AND DROPS IT ON THE FLOOR.

BETSY (cont'd)
What's that?

EMILY
A note.

BETSY
To who?

EMILY
I don't know. I don't pass notes.

BETSY
What, are you trying to tempt me or something?

EMILY
No.

BETSY
'Cause you know I'm not like you. I could care less what
that note says.

EMILY

Sure.

A BEAT.

BETSY

Is there actually anything on that paper?

EMILY

Why do you care?

BETSY

I don't. I was just asking.

EMILY

(Tempting her) It's killing you isn't it?

BETSY

No.

EMILY

You're dying to find out what's in that note.

BETSY JUMPS ON THE FLOOR AND GRABS THE NOTE.

EMILY (cont'd)

Ha. I knew it.

BETSY

(Looking at the paper) This is your math homework!

EMILY

You're sad.

BETSY

We're both sad.

EMILY

Got any more gum?

BETSY

Yeah. But you'll have to write me a note first.

Big Trouble

INT. CHARLIE'S BEDROOM

JOHNNY IS SITTING ON HIS BED PLAYING VIDEO GAMES
WHEN CHARLIE WALKS IN.

> CHARLIE
> Oh dude, I heard. I'm sooo sorry.

> JOHNNY
> Heard what?

> CHARLIE
> That Chip Underwood is going to beat you up.

> JOHNNY
> No!

> CHARLIE
> Yeah, I heard him talking after football practice. He's really
> mad.

> JOHNNY
> Why? I didn't do anything to him.

> CHARLIE
> He says you've been talkin' trash about him. Saying he's
> only on the football team 'cause his dad's the coach.

> JOHNNY
> It's the truth. You even said that.

> CHARLIE
> Yeah, but he didn't hear me say it. He wants to meet you
> after school tomorrow.

> JOHNNY
> I'm not fighting Underwood. He's twice my size.

> CHARLIE
> Oh, you'll fight him. Maybe not tomorrow. But Chip's
> mean. He'll track you down. And then you're in big trou-
> ble.

> JOHNNY
> Oh man. This bites. What am I going to do?

> CHARLIE
> (Thinking) Well—let me see.

JOHNNY
Charlie you got to think of something. I like my face the way it is. I don't want Chip to rearrange it.

CHARLIE
Okay, don't start crying.

JOHNNY
I wasn't crying.

CHARLIE
You will be once Chip sees you.

Swimming For Love

<u>EXT. THE FRONT PORCH OF MORGANA'S HOUSE</u>

JORDAN AND MORGANA ARE IN THE MIDDLE OF A
CONVERSATION.

> JORDAN
> Just friends?

> MORGANA
> I'm sorry. I just don't feel the same way about you that you feel
> about me.

> JORDAN
> (In shock) Just friends?!

> MORGANA
> I'm sorry. You're a nice guy.

> JORDAN
> Oh, don't say that.

> MORGANA
> It's true. You're sweet and...

> JORDAN
> Sweet? Please, you've hurt me enough already.

> MORGANA
> Jordan, you're just not my type.

> JORDAN
> You're type? I'm the first guy you've ever dated. You don't have a
> type.

> MORGANA
> Maybe not. But I'm pretty sure you're not it.

A BEAT.

> JORDAN
> Okay. Now that really hurt.

> MORGANA
> I'm sorry. I like you but...

JORDAN

But what?

MORGANA

I don't like-like you.

JORDAN

Hey, one like's good enough for me.

MORGANA

You're funny.

JORDAN

You're beautiful.

MORGANA

(Laughing) Jordan...

JORDAN

I can't help it. I like-like you.

MORGANA

No, you don't.

JORDAN

I do. I might even like-like-like you.

MORGANA

You're being silly.

JORDAN

I can't help it. You make me crazy.

MORGANA

Jordan!

JORDAN

You do. All week I haven't been able to think of anything but your eyes. I sit in class dreaming of your smile. I go to sleep thinking of your laugh. I spend hours trying to do my homework but I can do nothing but write your name. Face it Morgana, I'm crazy about you.

MORGANA

You're making this really hard.

JORDAN

Good. Dumping somebody shouldn't be easy.

MORGANA

I'm not dumping you. We can still be friends.

JORDAN

Stop saying that! I've got friends. What I need is a girl.

MORGANA

I...can't.

JORDAN

Then I'm going to have to stand on your porch all night until you change your mind.

MORGANA

(Laughing) You will not.

JORDAN

Try me.

MORGANA

You'd do it, too.

JORDAN

For you I would walk across the desert. Swim the Pacific ocean. Eat the food from the lunch room.

MORGANA

No, not that!

JORDAN

I would even eat the meatloaf!

MORGANA

Wow. You really do like-like-like me.

JORDAN

You bet ya.

MORGANA

Then to save you from a fate worse than death, I better agree to go out with you again.

JORDAN

You will?

MORGANA

How about Saturday?

JORDAN

I can't. I'm swimming the Pacific ocean for my new girlfriend.

MORGANA

(Throwing her arms around him) You're so crazy.

Same Thing

INT. THE GYM

CINDY AND LESLIE ARE DECORATING FOR THE DANCE. THEY ARE BOTH CHEWING GUM.

>   CINDY
> This is going to be the best dance ever.
>
>   LESLIE
> No, it's going to be better than the best dance ever!
>
>   CINDY
> How can it be better?
>
>   LESLIE
> Because this time I have a date! (Putting up a poster) Hand me the tape.
>   CINDY
> We're out.
>
>   LESLIE
> Oh, well. (Leslie takes her gum and puts it on the back of the poster.) That should stick.
>
>   CINDY
> What are you wearing?
>
>   LESLIE
> I got this great dress at Macy's.
>
>   CINDY
> (Trying to hang a poster) I got my dress at Macy's too.
>
>   LESLIE
> They have great stuff. (Looking at Cindy's poster) That's not straight.
>
>   CINDY
> (Straightening the poster) You're so good at decorating. I'm so glad we had a chance to work together on the dance committee.
>
>   LESLIE
> Me, too.
>
>   CINDY
> I've seen you around school for like forever. But I never had a chance to talk to you.

LESLIE
Same here. Good thing we're juniors. We have a whole
year left to be friends. (Holding up a piece of ribbon) Hey,
this ribbon is the color of my dress.

CINDY
Mine, too. Well, maybe a little darker.

LESLIE
(Stops decorating) You're wearing a red dress too?

CINDY
(Still decorating) I think the color is more cherry.

LESLIE
Cherry? Does it have a V neck?

CINDY
Yeah.

LESLIE
With short sleeves?

CINDY
Yes. It's really cute.

LESLIE
And lace on the bottom?

CINDY
Lots of lace.

LESLIE
(Screaming) Ahhhhh!

CINDY
What?!

LESLIE
We're wearing the same dress. The <u>exact</u> same dress.

CINDY
It just shows we both have good taste.

LESLIE
We can't both wear the same dress. We'll look like twins.

CINDY
No we won't. You are much better looking than me. You'll
be Cinderella. I'll look like your ugly stepsister.

LESLIE
(Laughing) You will not. <u>You'll</u> be Cinderella and I'll look
like one of the horses.

CINDY
(Laughing) So what if we have on the same dress. Guys never notice what you're wearing anyway. Hand me the scissors.

LESLIE
(She does) Yeah. Once my mom, who has always had really long hair, got it cut short. My dad didn't say anything for a month. And by that time it had grown out.

CINDY
I believe it. We could both wear garbage bags and our dates wouldn't even care.

LESLIE
I know Skeeter won't. Every time I'm with him, he's always looking at the floor. He's so shy.

CINDY
Hey, I'm dating a guy named Skeeter, too. (Holding up a new poster) Does this look straight to you?

LESLIE
(Ripping down Cindy's poster) No, it is not straight!

CINDY
You don't have to get all mad about it.

LESLIE
SKETTER? HOW COULD YOU COME TO THE DANCE WITH A GUY NAMED SKEETER?

CINDY
Well, he asked me. Isn't that cool that both our boyfriends have the same name?

LESLIE
NO! IT IS NOT COOL!!!

CINDY
I think it is.

LESLIE
CINDY WAKE UP! We are dating the same guy!!!

CINDY
Oh, that's not good.

LESLIE
We are wearing the same dress to the same dance dating the same guy.

CINDY
I knew we had a lot in common.

Caveboy

INT. THE KITCHEN

GARRISON IS SITTING AT THE DINNER TABLE. HE IS STARING AT AN EMPTY BOWL WHEN UGH SAUNTERS IN. HE LOOKS EXHAUSTED. *(NOTE UGH IS A CAVEBOY AND DOESN'T SPEAK ENG-LISH. HE JUST GRUNTS. HAVE FUN WITH THE GRUNTS. DON'T COPY THE EXACT WORDS I'VE WRITTEN FOR HIM. MAKE UP YOUR OWN LANGUAGE.)*

> GARRISON
> Good morning.

> UGH
> (Grunts) Ugh.

> GARRISON
> Late night?

> UGH
> Ugh.

UGH REACHES FOR THE BOX OF CEREAL.

> GARRISON
> We're out of cereal.

> UGH
> Ugh.

UGH GOES TO THE FRIDGE.

> GARRISON
> We're out of eggs, too.

> UGH
> (Sitting back down) Ugh!

> GARRISON
> Mom says she's not buying anymore food until we start treating her with respect.

UGH

Ugh!

GARRISON

Yeah, I agree. I tried to tell her Cave people don't understand respect.

UGH

(Agreeing) Ugh.

GARRISON

But she said, you may have been a caveboy twelve thousand years ago. But now that you've thawed out, you better learn some manners.

UGH

(Angry) Ugh! Ugh! Ugh!

GARRISON

Hey, don't blame me. Mom's the one who said it.

UGH

Ugh.

GARRISON

You know she's kind of right. Your eating habits are gross.

UGH

(Going wild) Ugh! Ugh! Ugh!

GARRISON

It's true! Every time you eat, you get food all over your face. All over the table. All over the floor. I think there's some spaghetti on the ceiling.

UGH

(Humiliated) Ugh.

GARRISON

Manners aren't that hard to learn. If you want, I can teach you.

UGH

Ugh!

GARRISON

Then forget it. We'll just starve to death.

UGH

(Giving in) Ugh.

GARRISON

Okay, here we go. Let's start with the silverware. This is a fork.

GARRISON MIMES EATING.

>   UGH
>   (Pretending to eat) Fooork.
>
>   GARRISON
>   Good. You've got it.
>
>   UGH
>   (Excited) Ugh! Ugh!!!
>
>   GARRISON
>   Okay, don't get excited!

UGH SITS DOWN AND STARTS SCRATCHING HIS HEAD WITH HIS FORK.

>   GARRISON (cont'd)
>   And never scratch your head with your fork. That's dis-
>   gusting!
>
>   UGH
>   Ugh!
>
>   GARRISON
>   Give me that. You can't eat with a dirty fork. Now here's a
>   spoon.

UGH USES THE SPOON TO SCRATCH UNDER HIS ARMPIT.

>   GARRISON (cont'd)
>   This is going to be harder than I thought.

Better Than You

EXT. THE TRACK FIELD

JACKIE COMES RUNNING IN.

> JACKIE
> I won!

ROGER COMES TRAILING BEHIND. HE IS EXHAUSTED.

> ROGER
> Man, you're fast.

> JACKIE
> No, you're just slow. Now do you believe me? Everything you can do, I can do better.

> ROGER
> Lets do the pushups again.

> JACKIE
> I beat you in pushups three times already today.

> ROGER
> Bet you can't make it four.

> JACKIE
> You're on! But you go first.

ROGER LIES DOWN ON THE FLOOR. HE TRIES TO PUSH UP WITH ALL HIS MIGHT.

> ROGER
> Ah!!!

HE ONLY MAKES IT UP HALFWAY. HE THEN FALLS FLAT ON HIS FACE.

> JACKIE
> (Laughing) A half? That's your best? A half?

> ROGER
> I'm tired.

JACKIE
You're weak. My turn. One, two...

JACKIE JUMPS ON THE FLOOR AND DOES TWO PUSHUPS.

ROGER
Okay, you win.

JACKIE
Look, I didn't even break a sweat. Okay admit it, I can do everything better than you.

ROGER
What about arm wrestling? I'm great at arm wrestling.

JACKIE
Please. With your little skinny arms you won't last three seconds.

ROGER
(Getting in the arm wrestling position) Them's fighting words.

JACKIE
(Taking his hand) One, two, three.

JACKIE EASILY SLAMS ROGER'S HAND DOWN. ROGER
FALLS ON THE FLOOR.

JACKIE (cont'd)
Are you okay?

ROGER
I wasn't ready.

JACKIE
You want to try again?

ROGER
(Not able to get up) That's okay.

JACKIE
Then I'm the winner. The champion of the world! Yes!!! I told you I could beat you.

ROGER
I wasn't ready.

JACKIE
Admit it. Everything you can do I can do better.

ROGER
Wait, there is one thing I can do better than you.

JACKIE
You're crazy. Every contest we've tried, I've won. Tennis. I won. Golf. I won. Badminton. I won. Swimming. Running. Pushups. Arm wrestling. I won, won, won!

ROGER
Okay. Okay. You're great at all of those things.

JACKIE
Great?

ROGER
The best. I admit it. But there is still one thing I can do better than you.

JACKIE
Impossible.

ROGER
(Holding out his hand) You want to bet?

JACKIE
(Shaking his hand) What do we bet?

ROGER
The loser has to carry the winner home.

JACKIE
It's a deal. So what do you think you can do better than me?

ROGER
Kiss.

A BEAT.

JACKIE
(Laughing) Kiss?

ROGER
I'm a great kisser.

JACKIE
Who told you that?

ROGER
I just know it. I've been practicing.

ROGER KISSES HIS ARM.

JACKIE
That's not a pretty sight. Look, I'm not kissing you.

ROGER
Then I win. Yes!!! (Really teasing her) Admit it. I can do something better than you.

JACKIE
(Getting mad) No, you can't! Okay let's kiss. I'm a better kisser than you are.

ROGER LEANS IN TO KISS HER.

JACKIE (cont'd)
(Stopping him) Wait. How do we tell who's the best?

ROGER
Oh, you'll know.

ROGER GENTLY KISSES JACKIE. IT ONLY LASTS A SECOND. BUT JACKIE IS DEEPLY EFFECTED.

JACKIE
(Holding her arms out) Hop on.

ROGER JUMPS IN TO JACKIE'S ARMS AND SHE CARRIES HIM OFF.

Stupid Ideas

<u>EXT. IN FRONT OF THE SCHOOL</u>

LIBBY AND JANE ARE LEAVING SCHOOL. LIBBY IS SO HAPPY THAT SHE'S FLOATING ON AIR.

> JANE
> (Very upset) Greg asked you out?

> LIBBY
> Yep!

> JANE
> Just like that?

> LIBBY
> Just like that. He looked at me with those beautiful blue eyes and...

> JANE
> (Getting more upset) And what?

> LIBBY
> ...he asked me out!

> JANE
> But I thought he liked me.

> LIBBY
> I thought he did, too.

> JANE
> He's always smiling at me, telling me how beautiful I look. And he's always standing by my locker when I come out of gym.

> LIBBY
> Well that's the problem.

> JANE
> What is?

> LIBBY
> He saw you after gym. Greg hates sweat.

> JANE
> Sweat?

LIBBY
Hates it. Before he asked me out, you know what he said?
"Libby the best thing about you is, you don't sweat."

JANE
That's stupid. I've seen him after gym and he's covered
with sweat.

LIBBY
I know, isn't he cute? But he's a boy. Boys sweat.

JANE
Well, so do girls.

LIBBY
Maybe but not girls that Greg wants to go out with. Oh,
but that's not the only reason he likes me better than you.
Greg told me he hates how you make good grades in
math.

JANE
What's wrong with good grades?

LIBBY
Greg says you're a show off. He says everyone knows boys
are smarter than girls. Especially in math. And so you, by
making better grades than him, are just showing off.

JANE
That's the stupidest thing I've ever heard.

LIBBY
He told me you would say that.

JANE
He did?

LIBBY
Greg said you always think everybody's ideas are stupid.
Except for yours of course.

JANE
(Getting really mad) I do not!

LIBBY
Hey, don't get mad at me! Greg said it.

JANE
Well, Greg is stupid! Stupid! Stupid! Stupid! I can't believe I
ever liked such a stupid person. Did he say anything else
about me?

LIBBY
Oh, yeah. Tons of stuff. (Pulling a note out of her pocket) He wrote it all down in this note.

JANE
(Grabbing the note) Give me that! (Reading) "Dear Libby, Please tell your sister that I like her and want her to go to the prom with me. I am too shy to ask her myself. Every time I get close to her, I get all goofy. She is so smart and pretty. Why can't all girls be as great as Jane? Thank you, Greg."

LIBBY
(Laughing) Isn't he so stupid?

Sensational Comedic Scenes

She Likes Me!

INT. THE LUNCHROOM

JAMIE AND TY ARE SITTING ACROSS FROM EACH OTHER EATING
LUNCH. JAMIE LOOKS UP.

> JAMIE
> Don't turn around but she's looking over here!

> TY
> (Turning around) Who is?

> JAMIE
> Don't turn around!

> TY
> (Turning back) How am I suppose to see...?

> JAMIE
> She's so beautiful.

> TY
> Who is?

> JAMIE
> She's waving.

JAMIE WAVES BACK.

> TY
> Who are you talking about?

> JAMIE
> (Laughing and waving again) She is so beautiful when she does that.

> TY
> Does what?

> JAMIE
> (Shocked) Oh my god, I can't believe she did that.

> TY
> Did what?

> JAMIE
> (Upset) Well, forget her.

> **TY**
> How can I forget her when I don't even know who you're talking about.

> **JAMIE**
> She's waving again. I think she's sorry. Should I forgive her?

> **TY**
> For what? Forgive her for what?!

> **JAMIE**
> She's leaving. Should I follow her?

> **TY**
> Follow who?

> **JAMIE**
> I've got to do it. She's the girl of my dreams. She's the girl of every guy's dream.

JAMIE RUNS OFF.

> **TY**
> (Finally turning around) Next time, I'm sitting at another table.

Cheater

<u>INT. SCIENCE CLASS</u>

CATHIE AND PETE ARE TAKING A BIOLOGY TEST. PETE IS TRYING TO CHEAT OFF CATHIE'S TEST.

                    CATHIE
(Whispering) Stop looking at my paper!

                    PETE
What's the answer to question five?

                    CATHIE
(Outraged) I'm not telling.

                    PETE
Come on. Please.

                    CATHIE
No! You should have studied.

                    PETE
I did. But I didn't know the "parts of a plant" were going to be on the test.

                    CATHIE
I studied them anyway.

                    PETE
Please.

                    CATHIE
No! I do not cheat.

                    PETE
Forget it. By the way, you got the answer to question two wrong.

                    CATHIE
Did not.

                    PETE
Did too. (Reading question two) Where do bees live? Think about it.

                    CATHIE
Combs. Bees live in <u>combs</u>. Haven't you ever heard of honey combs?

PETE
Yes. It's a cereal. But bees live in <u>hives</u>.

CATHIE
(Erasing her answer) You're right. How could I have for-
gotten that?

PETE
It's easy. Sometimes in the middle of a test you just forget
things.

CATHIE
Thanks.

PETE
You're welcome.

A BEAT. PETE CLEARS HIS THROAT TO GET CATHIE'S
ATTENTION. SHE PRETENDS NOT TO NOTICE. HE CLEARS IT
AGAIN. SHE STILL DOESN'T NOTICE. THEN HE CLEARS IT
AGAIN, THIS TIME VERY LOUD.

CATHIE
Are you okay?

PETE
No, I'm not okay. I need the answer to question five.

CATHIE
I told you, I don't cheat.

PETE
But I just gave you the answer to question two.

CATHIE
I said thank you. What more do you want?

PETE
(Starting to get upset) The answer to question five!

CATHIE
Sorry.

PETE
Can you give me a hint?

CATHIE
Nope.

PETE
Not even a little hint?

> CATHIE

No.

> PETE

Not even a little teenie weenie hint?

> CATHIE

No! I am not helping you cheat!

> PETE

Okay you asked for it. (Standing up) Mrs. Knapp, Cathie is trying to cheat off my paper!

> CATHIE

(Standing up) I am not!

> PETE

Yes, she is. Look at her test. On question two she wrote down "comb" and then she looked over at my paper and saw the answer was "hive", so she erased her answer. Cathie admit it! You cheated!

> CATHIE

(Sitting down) Oh brother.

The List

EXT. THE BLEACHERS AROUND THE FOOTBALL FIELD

RACHEL IS SITTING READING A SINGLE SHEET OF PAPER. HEIDI WALKS UP.

> **HEIDI**
> There you are.

> **RACHEL**
> (Depressed) Hey.

> **HEIDI**
> What's wrong?

> **RACHEL**
> Did you see this?

> **HEIDI**
> What is it?

> **RACHEL**
> It's the popular list.

> **HEIDI**
> What's that?

> **RACHEL**
> My brother told me about it. Every year popular people get together and make a list of who's popular and who's not.

> **HEIDI**
> Sounds kind of stupid.

> **RACHEL**
> Yeah, I guess.

> **HEIDI**
> So you're not on it?

> **RACHEL**
> That's not the problem.

RACHEL HANDS HEIDI THE LIST.

> **HEIDI**
> (Excited) You're number one! You're the most popular person in the whole school!!!

RACHEL
(Sarcastic) Whoopee.

HEIDI
And look, I'm number two! I didn't even know anybody knew me.

RACHEL
They don't.

HEIDI
But I'm number two.

RACHEL
That's not the real list. The real list comes out tomorrow and since I knew we wouldn't be on it, I made a fake list.

HEIDI
Brilliant. Rachel, you are a genius!

RACHEL
It'll never work. I just did it to make myself feel better.

HEIDI
Are you kidding? Of course it will work. My dad's got a copy machine at his office. We'll make a thousand copies and put one in everybody's locker.

RACHEL
But the popular people are going to know it's not the real list.

HEIDI
Who cares. The unpopular people won't.

RACHEL
But what good is that?

HEIDI
It's brilliant. See, if the unpopular people think they are now popular, then they are going to treat the popular people as unpopular. And then, the popular people will get upset and act stupid. And then they'll really be unpopular. And then, the original unpopular people will be popular for making the popular people unpopular.

RACHEL
Oh-my-god, it is brilliant!

HEIDI
(Giving her a big hug) Rachel, you're a genius.

Whoops

EXT. CORBIN'S YARD

CORBIN IS HOLDING A GARAGE SALE.

> **CORBIN**
> (Yelling to the crowd) Video games! Get your video games!

HUGHSTON ENTERS. HE IS A LOT BIGGER THAN CORBIN.

> **HUGHSTON**
> Hey Corbin. What's up?

> **CORBIN**
> Nothing. Just having a garage sale. (To the crowd) Video games! Great selection!

> **HUGHSTON**
> Why are you selling all your stuff?

> **CORBIN**
> I need some money for a new bike. (To the crowd) Playstation 2! Dreamcast! N64! Get'em while they're hot!

> **HUGHSTON**
> I can't believe it. You've always been obsessed with video games. (Looking at Corbin's games) Hey, isn't this my Final Fantasy 9?

> **CORBIN**
> Is it?

> **HUGHSTON**
> (Aggravated) Yeah. It has my name right here.

> **CORBIN**
> (Getting nervous) Oh. Take it then.

> **HUGHSTON**
> Wait, this is my Goldeneye game, too.

> **CORBIN**
> Really?

> **HUGHSTON**
> And this is my Zelda cartridge! Look, here is my Perfect Dark game! In fact all of these games are mine!!!

CORBIN
Okay, okay you caught me. Your mom gave them to me.

HUGHSTON
(Starts moving toward Corbin) My parents are on vacation in Hawaii.

CORBIN
(Backing up) Yeah, well she called me from Hawaii and told me to go in your room and get your games. She's tired of you playing them in the house.

HUGHSTON
Am I supposed to believe that?

HUGHSTON STARTS CHASING CORBIN.

CORBIN
(Running) Well how about this? Last night I was sleepwalking and I must have gone into your house and accidentally walked off with your games. Yeah, that's it.

HUGHSTON
If I catch you, you're dead.

CORBIN
It's a good thing you walked by. I almost sold all your stuff. I better call the doctor and see if he can help me with my sleepwalking. In fact I better see him now!

CORBIN RUNS OFF.

HUGHSTON
Oh, you're going to need a doctor all right!

HUGHSTON RUNS AFTER HIM.

Flying Accusations

<u>EXT. THE PARK</u>

CYNTHIA AND ANDREW ARE IN THE MIDDLE OF A FIGHT.

> **CYNTHIA**
> I am <u>not</u> in love with Frankie!

> **ANDREW**
> I didn't say you were in <u>love</u> with him. But there is definite-
> ly something between you.

> **CYNTHIA**
> There is not! You and Frankie are best friends! I am not
> going to cheat on you with your best friend.

> **ANDREW**
> Oh. But you would cheat on me with someone else?!

> **CYNTHIA**
> Andy, listen to you. What are you doing?

> **ANDREW**
> Don't ask me. You are the one who's cheating.

> **CYNTHIA**
> Are you trying to make me mad so I'll break up with you?
> 'Cause it's working.

> **ANDREW**
> No you're not breaking up with me. I'm breaking up with you!

> **CYNTHIA**
> I didn't say I wanted to break up.

> **ANDREW**
> Then why are you in love with Frankie?

> **CYNTHIA**
> (Getting really upset) I am not in love with Frankie!!!

> **ANDREW**
> Well, that's what he told me.

> **CYNTHIA**
> (Laughing) He did not.

> **ANDREW**
> He did! He said you better watch Cynthia. I think she's in
> love with me.

CYNTHIA
He was joking. Was he laughing when he said it?

ANDREW
Yeah.

CYNTHIA
That means he's kidding. Laughing. Kidding. Get it?

ANDREW
So, you're not in love with Frankie?

CYNTHIA
For the millionth time, no.

ANDREW
Then why are you cheating on me?

CYNTHIA
I'm not! You're driving me crazy!!!

ANDREW
So, if you're not cheating, why did you break up with me?

CYNTHIA
You broke up with me.

ANDREW
I did?

CYNTHIA
Yes.

ANDREW
Oh. You want to go out with me again?

CYNTHIA
Only if you promise to stop accusing me of being in love with Frankie.

ANDREW
Okay. But you have to promise me you won't get mad about Rhonda.

CYNTHIA
Who's Rhonda?

ANDREW
The girl I'm cheating on you with.

CYNTHIA
You better be kidding.

ANDREW
I am. But now you see how it feels.

CYNTHIA
Ah!!!!!!!!!!!

Wrong Date (part 1)

<u>INT. THE GIRL'S BATHROOM</u>

BETHANY BOUNCES INTO THE ROOM. SHE GOES TO THE MIRROR AND STARTS BRUSHING HER HAIR. HANNAH DRAGS IN.

>   HANNAH
> Why do girls always have to go the bathroom together?
>
>   BETHANY
> It gives us a chance to talk about the boys.
>
>   HANNAH
> You're sooo boy crazy. This is the last double date I'm ever going on with you.
>
>   BETHANY
> You don't like Philip?
>
>   HANNAH
> How should I know?! He's been talking to you all night.
>
>   BETHANY
> He's so funny.
>
>   HANNAH
> I think Brandon is getting mad that you're ignoring him.
>
>   BETHANY
> I'm not ignoring him. I'm just trying to make Philip feel comfortable.
>
>   HANNAH
> But Philip is my date.
>
>   BETHANY
> I know that. Brush your hair. It's getting all frizzy.
>
>   HANNAH
> It looks fine.
>
>   BETHANY
> (Brushing Hannah's hair) You look like a clown.
>
>   HANNAH
> Ow! (Taking the brush) Here, let me do it.

BETHANY STARTS REAPPLYING HER LIPSTICK.

BETHANY
I wish Brandon was as funny as Philip.

HANNAH
Philip's not funny. He's stupid.

BETHANY
What?

HANNAH
He makes all those jokes about South Park. That show is
so for losers.

BETHANY
I think it's funny.

HANNAH
And what was that story he told about playing video
games? He's sixteen and he's still playing video games?

BETHANY
I have a Playstation.

HANNAH
Your date is much better. Brandon likes to read poetry,
hike in the woods...

BETHANY
How boring.

HANNAH
He told me he's a huge U2 fan. Remember last year when I
saw them in concert? He was there, too.

BETHANY
Uh. Oh.

HANNAH
What?

BETHANY
We're with the wrong guys. You should be with Brandon.
And Philip with me.

HANNAH
You're right.

BETHANY
What do we do about it?

HANNAH
Nothing. What can we do?

BETHANY
There's got to be something. (A beat) I've got it. I am so
bad.

HANNAH
Forget it! I don't want to do any of your crazy ideas.

BETHANY
You can pretend that you're sick. And since Brandon lives
close to you, he can take you home.

HANNAH
But that's lying.

BETHANY
So what?

HANNAH
I don't want to start off our relationship with a lie.

BETHANY
If you don't lie, there's not going to be a relationship.

HANNAH
I don't know.

BETHANY
Okay then. You want to go out there and say, 'Listen boys
we've been thinking. I think we're with the wrong dates?'

HANNAH
That would not be good.

BETHANY
So pretend that you're sick.

HANNAH
Why do I let you talk me into these things?

BETHANY
Call me tomorrow and tell me if he kisses you?

HANNAH
I don't kiss and tell.

BETHANY
(Messing up her hair) Here, you've got to look sick.

HANNAH
I hope this works.

BETHANY
It will. Boys aren't as smart as they think they are.

Wrong Date (part II)

INT. A RESTAURANT

PHILIP AND BRANDON ARE SITTING AT A TABLE FOR FOUR.

BRANDON
Why do girls always have to go the bathroom together?

PHILIP
So we can talk about them. Hey bud, I really appreciate you setting me up tonight.

BRANDON
I bet you do. Bethany's talking to you more than me.

PHILIP
Don't get paranoid. Your girlfriend is not flirting with me.

BRANDON
She is too. Everything you say she dies laughing.

PHILIP
She did like my South Park impressions. But I don't think Hannah did.

BRANDON
Hannah's too cool for South Park.

PHILIP
She seems kind of stuck up.

BRANDON
Hannah's great. She's smart and we like a lot of the same bands. I wish Bethany was a little more like her.

PHILIP
Then let's switch.

BRANDON
What?

PHILIP
Look, you like the girl I'm with. And I like the girl you're with. Let's switch.

BRANDON
But Bethany's my girlfriend. You're on a blind date.

PHILIP
You've only been dating her a week.

BRANDON
I don't know.

PHILIP
Oh, come on. Did you see Hannah's eyes when you told her you write poetry?

BRANDON
Read poetry. I don't write it.

PHILIP
Whatever. She was into it.

BRANDON
Hannah is kind of cute. What am I doing? No! It would be wrong.

PHILIP
Okay, fine. You'll take Bethany home and I'll take Hannah. But the whole time you're going to be thinking of Hannah.

BRANDON
Okay. Let's do it. But how?

PHILIP
We could just tell them.

BRANDON
We could also bang our heads against the wall.

PHILIP
All right. How about if we pretend like you're sick. And Hannah lives close to you. And she can drive your car back home.

BRANDON
What about Bethany?

PHILIP
I'll be the big hero and offer to take Bethany home.

BRANDON
This will never work.

PHILIP
Sure it will. Girls aren't as smart as they think they are.

Homecoming

<u>EXT. OUTSIDE OF SCHOOL</u>

LISA IS WAITING FOR HER MOM TO PICK HER UP. EVAN RUNS IN.

> EVAN
>
> Hey Lisa.

> LISA
>
> Hey.

> EVAN
>
> So what do you think?

> LISA
>
> About what?

> EVAN
>
> You don't know? Oh, I thought someone would have told you by now.

> LISA
>
> Sorry, I haven't heard anything.

> EVAN
>
> I can't believe this! I had it all worked out. I told Ellie first. You know cause she rides to school with Katherine. And then Katherine and Taila have P.E. together. So I had that all covered. And then Taila and Lynn's lockers are right next to each other. And we just got out of fifth period when you and Lynn have Math so...I thought you'd know by now.

> LISA
>
> Sorry. Oh wait. Lynn gave me this note before I left class but I haven't read it yet.

> EVAN
>
> (Walking away) Uh-oh, gotta go!

> LISA
>
> (Grabbing his arm) Not so fast. (Reading) "Dear Lisa. I just heard from Taila who heard from Katherine who heard from Ellie who heard from Evan that he was going to ask you to homecoming. What are you going to say? Lynn." (To Evan) Is this true?

> EVAN
>
> It's true.

> LISA
>
> Wow. You went to a lot of trouble.

> EVAN
>
> You don't even know.

A BEAT.

> EVAN (cont'd)
>
> So?

> LISA
>
> So what?

> EVAN
>
> So...will you go to the homecoming with me?

> LISA
>
> I don't know, I have to think about it.

A BEAT.

> LISA (cont'd)
>
> Okay...I've decided.

> EVAN
>
> Well?

> LISA
>
> I'm not going to just tell you. I'll tell Lynn. And she'll tell Taila, who'll tell Katherine, who'll tell Ellie, who'll tell you.

> EVAN
>
> Oh man. What have I done?

Your Personal Angel

INT. SCHOOL HALLWAY

SWANNIE IS PUTTING HER BOOKS IN HER LOCKER WHEN KIKI
WALKS UP. SHE IS HOLDING A SCROLL.

                    KIKI
Excuse me, I'm looking for (glancing at her scroll)...Swannie
Brooks?

                    SWANNIE
Do I know you?

                    KIKI
No. Now tell me, why didn't you study harder on your
Spanish test? If you make another bad grade, your mother is
going to kill you.

                    SWANNIE
Excuse me?

                    KIKI
You're already grounded for staying out late with Justin. I
don't know why you date him. He's is such a loser.

                    SWANNIE
How do you know all these things about me?

                    KIKI
I'm your guardian angel. Did I forget to mention that? My
memory is not what it used to be. That's what comes from
being on the job for a thousand years. Where are you
going?

                    SWANNIE
(Trying to sneak off) Nowhere, I was just...

                    KIKI
Don't lie to me. I'm an angel. Our halos come with built-in
lie detectors.

                    SWANNIE
(Very nervous) Look it was nice of you to come and see
me, but I've got a really big Spanish test.

SWANNIE STARTS WALKING AWAY.

KIKI
(Putting a spell on her.) HOLD IT!

SWANNIE FREEZES.

SWANNIE
What did you do to me? I can't move!

KIKI
(Walking around to face her) That's right. And you won't be able to until you listen to me.

SWANNIE
HELP! HELP!!!

KIKI MAKES A MAGICAL GESTURE. SWANNIE IS IMMEDIATELY MUTE.

KIKI
Now, that's better. Listen, I haven't got much time. I've got another client in New York who is thinking about getting his nose pierced and I've got to stop him before it's too late. So listen up. The last couple of months I've been watching you and I am not at all pleased with your behavior. You've been a bad, bad girl.

SWANNIE IS TRYING TO SPEAK TO DEFEND HERSELF.

KIKI (cont'd)
Excuses. Excuses. I've heard it all before. You have got to shape up. Treat your parents better. Why do you scream at your mother? And study! You're a smart girl. Aren't you a little bit embarrassed getting all those D's? And that boyfriend. He treats you terribly. I mean, come on. His breath would kill a dragon. Swannie, get a life! Now, do you have anything to say for yourself?

SWANNIE TRIES TO TALK.

KIKI (cont'd)
Wait. This will help.

KIKI MAKES A MAGICAL GESTURE AGAIN.

SWANNIE

That is totally not fair. My mother is always on my case.
My teachers hate me and it's not my boyfriend's fault he
has halitosis.

KIKI

You're right. I'm sorry I even brought it up. Okay, gotta go,
have a nice life.

SWANNIE

Wait. That's it? You come down here, tell me all the things
that are wrong with me. Then when I disagree you just...fly
away?

KIKI

Yeah, that's pretty much it. I can't help anyone who does-
n't want to be helped. Look, I've got to run. There's a
whole world out there who wants my guidance.

SWANNIE

Hold it! What's going to happen to me?

KIKI

You mean like your future?

SWANNIE

Yeah. What's my future?

KIKI

(Looking at her scroll) Well, let's see. If you continue on
the path you are on, you will...wow, this is really horrible.

SWANNIE

It is?

KIKI

Your life is going to be really ghastly. I'm glad I'm not you.

SWANNIE

What's going to happen to me?

KIKI

You really want to know? 'Cause it's bad! Real bad.

A BEAT.

SWANNIE

No I guess not.

KIKI

Smart choice. Well, I'll see you around. Good luck. You're
going to need it.

SWANNIE
Wait. What happens if I change? You know, study? Treat my mom better? Dump my loser boyfriend?

KIKI
(Looking at her scroll again.) Oh well, that's much better. That's amazing. I've never read a life this great before. Congratulations.

SWANNIE
Thank you. I think. It's really that good?

KIKI
Fantastic. I'm honored to be your guardian angel. Wait till the angels back home hear about this one.

SWANNIE
Then that's it. I have to change.

KIKI
Good choice.

SWANNIE
Thanks a lot...angel.

KIKI
Call me Kiki.

SWANNIE
Thanks a lot Kiki. I really appreciate you coming all the way here to...

KIKI
Don't mention it. Oh, by the way, you don't look good with green nail polish. It clashes with your eyes.

SWANNIE
I kind of like it.

KIKI
Fine. Be that way. Just don't blame me if one of your fingers falls off.

SWANNIE
Okay, I'll change it.

KIKI
Good idea. Well, got to go. New York is a long flight.

SWANNIE
What if I need to get in touch with you? What do I do?

KIKI
Nothing. But don't worry, I'll be watching you.

Old Fashioned

INT. CLEBOT'S BEDROOM

THE 23RD CENTURY. CLEBOT IS SITTING IN FRONT OF HIS XL7 COMPUTER TERMINAL WHEN SASHA MATERIALIZES.

> SASHA
> Okay, this better be good. I was right in the middle of my virtual reality massage.

> CLEBOT
> Sasha, thanks for coming over. I really need your help.

> SASHA
> I'm not over. This is a hologram of me.

> CLEBOT
> Wow! Did your family upgrade their software?

> SASHA
> Yeah, Pop got a new android and it's really good at space projection. You like my new outfit?

> CLEBOT
> You look good.

> SASHA
> You should see it in person. Okay, what do you need me for? I've got a flying lesson in fifteen.

> CLEBOT
> It's about Sophie.

> SASHA
> Oh, please, you're not still in love with that loser.

> CLEBOT
> Sophie is not a loser. She's just gravitationally challenged.

> SASHA
> I'll say. So far this month she has driven her new BMW spaceship into a building, a robot and two asteroids.

> CLEBOT
> The asteroids weren't her fault.

> SASHA
> Tell that to the police.

CLEBOT
Okay, she's clumsy. But I'm in love with her.

SASHA
This week. Last week you were in love with some chick from the Bangaton galaxy.

CLEBOT
Yeah. But she dumped me when she found out I only had two eyes.

SASHA
How many did she have?

CLEBOT
About a dozen.

SASHA
It must take her all day to put on mascara.

CLEBOT
Anyway, what do I do about Sophie? She doesn't even know I exist.

SASHA
Oh, she knows after you built that laser that spelled out her name.

CLEBOT
Too bad it burned a hole in the school ceiling.

SASHA
Look, if you like Sophie, just tell her.

CLEBOT
You mean like write her an E-mail? Or send over a Hallmark Hologram?

SASHA
No. Go over to her house.

CLEBOT
In person?

SASHA
Yeah. Face to face.

CLEBOT
I could never do that.

SASHA
Then you'll never have a girlfriend. Sophie doesn't care about your computer or your lasers, or how fast your spaceship goes. She only cares about you. As a boy.

CLEBOT
How do you know that?

SASHA
'Cause she told me.

CLEBOT
When?

SASHA
Just now. I have conference hologramming.

CLEBOT
She's listening to this?!

SASHA
Yep. Look, you two talk it out. My flying instructor is waiting. Ciao.

Advice

INT. THE KITCHEN

AVERY ENTERS. HIS MOM, BARBARA, IS MAKING MEATLOAF.

> AVERY
> Mom, I need some advice.

> BARBARA
> (In shock) What?

> AVERY
> I need some advice.

BARBARA MIMES HAVING A MASSIVE HEART ATTACK.
SHE FALLS ON THE FLOOR ROLLING AROUND.

> AVERY (cont'd)
> Very funny, Mom.

> BARBARA
> Avery, are you feeling okay? Let me feel your forehead.
> You're a little warm.

> AVERY
> I'm fine. I just need some advice.

> BARBARA
> I'm sorry, it's just been so long since you asked my opinion
> on anything.

> AVERY
> Well, sit down 'cause this is important.

BARBARA SITS.

> BARBARA
> I'm listening.

> AVERY
> Okay, I've been thinking...

BARBARA STARTS LAUGHING.

AVERY (cont'd)

What?

BARBARA

I'm sorry. I'm sorry. This is just so great, you and me sitting down having an actual conversation.

AVERY

What are you talking about? We talk.

BARBARA

No, we don't. I talk. You mainly grunt. I say, "Hey Avery, how was school?". You say, "Ugh". I say, "Avery how is your soccer team looking this year". You say, "Ugh". "Avery, you want hamburgers for dinner?". "Ugh".

AVERY

Okay, okay. We're talking now.

BARBARA

(Excited) I know, isn't it great?!

AVERY

Mom, can I tell you my problem?

BARBARA

(Suddenly serious) PROBLEM? Oh my gosh! I thought you just needed advice. Why didn't you tell me you had a problem?!!

AVERY

I'm trying.

BARBARA

I hope it's not your grades. If you've flunked Algebra again your father is going to...

AVERY

Mom, I got a B in Algebra.

BARBARA

(Shocked) You did?!

AVERY

B plus actually.

BARBARA

(Jumps up and gives him a hug) Son, you are so smart. I knew if you applied yourself you could do it.

AVERY

Mom! My problem?

BARBARA

(Sitting back down) Oh, I'm sorry. Go ahead.

AVERY
Okay. I'll just lay it out. I'm getting older and...

BARBARA
Don't remind me. I feel ancient already.

AVERY
Mom, you're not that old.

BARBARA
Please, I have one foot in the grave and the other on a banana peel.

AVERY
Well, you look good for your age.

BARBARA JUMPS UP TO GET A TISSUE.

BARBARA
(Starting to cry) You are so sweet. I am the luckiest mother in the world.

AVERY
Mom, don't cry.

BARBARA
I can't help it.

BARBARA, STILL CRYING, HUGS HIM AGAIN, BUT THIS TIME MUCH HARDER.

AVERY
Mom, you're choking me.

BARBARA
I can't help it. I love you so much. You are such a good young man.

AVERY
(Prying her arms from around his neck) Thank you. You are a good mom, too.

BARBARA
(Hugging him again as she cries very hard) Ahhhhhhhh!

AVERY
Mom, please, sit down.

BARBARA
(Sitting) I wish your father was as nice as you. But all he does all day is complain, complain, complain. The meat is too dry. The baked potato is too hard. The chocolate cake is burned. (Starting to get angry) Well, if he'd get me an oven that worked half way decent, maybe I could cook some food that everyone liked.

AVERY
Have you told him that?

BARBARA
(Stops crying) Uh...no. I don't think I have.

AVERY
Then why don't you explain it to him? Just sit him down and tell him how you really feel.

BARBARA
(Jumping up) You're right! I have never told him how I feel. (Hugging him again) Thanks son, you are the best. I'm going to march right in there and make your father turn off "Baywatch" and listen to me. Thanks for the advice.

BARBARA MARCHES OFF. AVERY SITS DOWN EXHAUSTED.

AVERY
Yeah, thanks for your help, too.

Workout

INT. THE GYM

HAL IS DOING SIT-UPS. PAUL IS HOLDING HIS LEGS.

> PAUL
> Nine hundred and ninety-eight, nine hundred and ninety-nine, one thousand!

> HAL
> That was easy!

> PAUL
> You're like a machine. Tomorrow at the state championships, you're going to kick some butt.

> HAL
> Paul. You know I don't like that kind of language.

> PAUL
> Sorry. You know for a boxer, you're kind of sensitive.

> HAL
> Just because I hit my opponent in the face, doesn't mean I don't like them.

> PAUL
> I guess. Now here's your jump rope. You need to do about thirty minutes.

HAL STARTS JUMPING ROPE.

> HAL
> I can't wait for tomorrow.

> PAUL
> You can't wait to win, huh?

> HAL
> No, it's not that. Win or lose, it doesn't matter to me. I just like to box.

> PAUL
> Do you know who your first match is with?

> HAL
> They sent me a schedule. It's in my bag. I haven't even looked at it.

PAUL OPENS HAL'S BAG AND PULLS OUT THE SCHEDULE.

PAUL
I can't believe it! Your first match is with Charlie Sprawls.
His parents and my parents are friends.

HAL
How old is he?

PAUL
He's a senior at Hillwood High.

HAL
Hillwood's program is weaker than ours.

PAUL
I don't know about that. I saw him at the YMCA last week.
He's got a great left hook.

HAL
Oh, I'm really scared.

PAUL
Oh, and he's fast, too.

HAL
As Ali said, "I float like a butterfly, sting like a bee".

PAUL
Charlie is undefeated.

HAL
Well, he hasn't seen my right jab yet.

PAUL
Charlie's good. The newspapers always pick him as the
favorite.

HAL STOPS JUMPING ROPE.

HAL
(Going wild) Oh yeah! Wait till I smash his face. We'll see
who the favorite is! (Sparring) Take that Charlie, and that.

HAL IS SPARRING LIKE CRAZY.

PAUL
It doesn't matter who wins or loses? Right.

Gangs

INT. THE BATHROOM

Bud is at the sink. He is cleaning a wound on his arm when his sister, Z, bursts in.

> Z
> Let me see it.

> BUD
> Leave me alone!

> Z
> (Grabbing his arm) Oooo! They cut you good.

> BUD
> Who told you?

> Z
> Who didn't? Well, that's what you get for joining a gang.

> BUD
> Shut up! We're not a gang.

> Z
> What, you think I'm stupid? The 57's are a gang. Everyone knows that.

> BUD
> Whatever.

> Z
> (Mimicking him) Whatever. What, you think you're cool now?

> BUD
> Get out of here.

> Z
> Mom finds out about this and you're dead.

Z starts to leave but Bud slams the door.

> BUD
> You tell her and you're dead.

Z

What, you <u>threatening</u> me? You going to get your boys to come over and take care of your little sister?

BUD

No, I'll do it myself.

Z

I can't believe you. You let those bunch of morons cut you with a knife so you could be a part of their stupid gang?

BUD

It's called initiation. You won't understand.

Z

Try me.

BUD

The 57's are cool.

BUD (cont'd)

They are. For once I'm part of something. I watch their back. They watch mine.

Z

They didn't watch Googie's back.

BUD

That's different.

Z

Why? 'Cause he died?

BUD

Look, I'm not going to get hurt.

Z

You might.

BUD

Z, I'm going to be okay.

Z

You promise?

BUD

Yeah. Don't tell mom.

Z

I can do what I want. Unlike you I don't need no stupid gang to tell me what to do. Give me your arm. You don't even know how to take care of yourself.

Caring

INT. THE SCHOOL BATHROOM

Kelly checks her face in the mirror. Amy walks in.

> AMY
> Hey.

> KELLY
> (Startled) Hi.

> AMY
> You okay? You look pale.

> KELLY
> I'm fine. (Starting to exit) I've got to hurry or I'll be late for health.

Amy steps in front of the door.

> AMY
> Kelly, I think you better sit down. You don't look so good.

> KELLY
> I'm fine. (Trying again to exit) See you in class.

> AMY
> (Stepping in front of the door again) You got any mouthwash?

> KELLY
> (Looking in her purse) Yeah. (Pulling out a big bottle) Here. Now will you excuse...

> AMY
> This is a huge bottle!

> KELLY
> Keep it. I got to run!

> AMY
> (Still not letting her leave) You must be really worried about fresh breath.

> KELLY
> Look Amy...

> AMY
> Yeah, I guess I would be too if I was always going in the bathroom to throw up.

Kelly just stands there stunned. After a beat.

> KELLY
> What are you talking about?

> AMY
> I've suspected for a couple of weeks. But yesterday, Cheryl told me she heard you throwing up after gym. And I was standing outside just now so...

> KELLY
> Yeah, well I haven't been feeling really well. Must be the flu or something.

> AMY
> Kelly. You have a problem. You need to get some help.

> KELLY
> I don't have a problem. I'm just sick.

> AMY
> You're right. Eating disorders are a sickness.

> KELLY
> Shut up!

> AMY
> It's true. Now you have two choices...

> KELLY
> (Pushing her way through) Stop trying to control my life.

> AMY
> (Grabbing her arm and pushing her back into the bathroom) Kelly! Wake up! You're sick. Now <u>you</u> can go tell the nurse, or <u>I'm</u> going to tell her for you. Either way, you're going to get some help.

A long beat.

> KELLY
> Why are you doing this?

> AMY
> Because I care. Because someone did it for me.

> KELLY
> What?

> AMY
> How do you think I knew the symptoms so well? Now, what's it going to be? Are you going to tell her or am I?

A Friend in Need

INT. AT SCHOOL IN FRONT OF ZIP'S LOCKER

Zip looks around and then puts something in his locker. Kirk sneaks up behind him.

> KIRK
>
> Hey dude!

Zip jumps and then slams his locker.

> ZIP
>
> Man, you scared me!

Kirk realizes he may have seen a weapon in Zip's locker.

> KIRK
>
> Was that a gun?
>
> ZIP
>
> (Playing innocent) What?
>
> KIRK
>
> Man, you brought a gun to school?
>
> ZIP
>
> Oh that, no man, it's just a toy. For drama class. You know like a prop.
>
> KIRK
>
> Let me see it.
>
> ZIP
>
> (Starting to walk off) Come on, we're going to be late for biology.

Kirk pushes Zip against the locker.

> KIRK
>
> Zip, are you crazy?! They'll expel you.
>
> ZIP
>
> I had to!

KIRK
Why?

ZIP
Some people are going to jump me.

KIRK
Who?

ZIP
Some guys in the 57's.

KIRK
Oh man. How did you get messed up with them?

ZIP
This one dude said I was looking at him wrong. He's hated
me ever since. So I brought the gun. This way they try to
jack me and I'm packin'.

KIRK
What're you going to do, shoot 'em? That's wacked! Zip,
you're carrying a deadly weapon. You shoot somebody
and you're going to jail forever.

ZIP
I'd rather be in jail than dead.

KIRK
I bet there's a lot of criminals that would disagree with
that.

ZIP
No ones going to jump me. I'm tired of being a wimp.

KIRK
Man, if you think carrying a gun makes you any less a wimp
you're wrong. If the school finds out you have a weapon,
you're out of here. You'll have to go to jail. And if you
think the gangs are bad in school, I hear the ones in jail are
worse.

ZIP
I'll take my chances.

KIRK
I can't believe you. Where did you get a gun anyway?

ZIP
My step-dad.

KIRK
He gave it to you?

ZIP
What do you think?

KIRK
Man, it's going to be lonely around here without you to kick it with.

ZIP
I'm not going anywhere.

KIRK
Oh yeah you are, 'cause I'm going to the office to turn you in. Now, if you come with me, they'll be a lot easier on you.

ZIP
Why are you doing this?

KIRK
'Cause I care about you. And I don't want to see you on the front of Time magazine as some crazy guy who went wild at school. Now come on, let's go.

Kirk exits. Zip doesn't move.

Grounded Big Time

INT. KATHRYN'S ROOM

Kathryn is doing her homework. Scott knocks.

> KATHRYN
> Go away!

> SCOTT
> (Whispering) It's me.

> KATHRYN
> Go away!

> SCOTT
> (Opening door) I'm sorry.

> KATHRYN
> Get out of here!

> SCOTT
> Don't be mad.

> KATHRYN
> Scott, I'm grounded for six weeks!!! No TV! No phone!
> No dates! Nothing!

> SCOTT
> Mom was really mad.

> KATHRYN
> She was screaming!

> SCOTT
> Then why didn't you tell her you didn't steal the money?

> KATHRYN
> 'Cause she would've known that you did.

> SCOTT
> I'm sorry.

> KATHRYN
> Don't tell me. Tell Mom.

> SCOTT
> I can't. She said the next time I steal something, she's going
> to make me sit in the yard holding a sign that says 'thief'.

> KATHRYN
> That would be embarrassing. Why do you steal anyway?

SCOTT
I don't know. 'Cause I need stuff. Everybody at school gets an allowance expect for us.

KATHRYN
Are you doing drugs?

SCOTT
No! I just wanna buy cool things like everybody else.

KATHRYN
But Dad says anytime we want money all we have to do is ask and...he'll give us a job to earn it.

SCOTT
It's no fair we have to work for our money.

KATHRYN
You think stealing isn't working? First you have to find the money. Then steal it. And then worry about getting caught. And then when you do get caught, and you always do, then you have to be punished. And then they make you give back all the money. So you go through all of that and you get nothing.

SCOTT
I never looked at it like that before.

KATHRYN
You could do one of Dad's jobs in half the time. And you'd get paid. And then you could ask him for another job and get paid more. I bet you'd have a lot more money than anybody else at school.

SCOTT
Yeah. You're right.

KATHRYN
Plus your sister wouldn't be grounded.

SCOTT
Can I borrow some paper and markers?

KATHRYN
What for?

SCOTT
I need to make a sign that says 'thief' on it.

KATHRYN
(Giving him a big hug) You're the best!

Hospital

INT. A HOSPITAL

Christy is sitting in a chair waiting. Penny rushes in and throws her arms around her sister.

> PENNY
> Christy!

> CHRISTY
> You made it!

> PENNY
> I got here as soon as I could. The bus was late. Mom out of surgery?

> CHRISTY
> No. And it's been three hours. Doctor Duncan said he'd come out and talk to us as soon as the surgery is over.

> PENNY
> Doctor Duncan? He's Mom's doctor?

> CHRISTY
> He was the only one on duty.

> PENNY
> Mom hates Doctor Duncan. I hate him, too.

> CHRISTY
> How do you think I feel? You weren't here. I tried to get somebody else. But the nurse wouldn't listen.

> PENNY
> Did you tell her Doctor Duncan killed our dad?

> CHRISTY
> He didn't kill Dad!

> PENNY
> He was the doctor when Dad died in the hospital.

> CHRISTY
> I told her that. But she said Doctor Duncan was the only one on duty and Mom needed help now.

> PENNY
> He gives me the creeps. What happened?

CHRISTY
When I got home from school, I found her unconscious. She was just lying on the ground in the garden. I checked to see if she was breathing. She wasn't.

PENNY
Oh no!

CHRISTY
So I gave her mouth to mouth. Mrs. Cahill was driving by and she saw what I was doing and called the ambulance from her car phone.

PENNY
I guess being nosey finally paid off.

CHRISTY
They got there really fast. They put Mom on one of those machines and....

Christy breaks down. Penny puts her arms around her.

PENNY
You did good kid. You did good.

CHRISTY
I was so scared.

PENNY
Mom will be proud. Where did you learn mouth-to-mouth?

CHRISTY
Health class.

PENNY
Good thing you were paying attention. You probably saved her life.

CHRISTY
You think so?

PENNY
Look, here comes Doctor Duncan.

CHRISTY
And he's smiling.

PENNY
(Whispering) What does that mean?

CHRISTY
Let's hope it doesn't mean he killed her.

Pay Up

EXT. THE FOOTBALL FIELD

Mark is hiding behind a gate when Chris enters. Mark grabs Chris.

> MARK
> Gotcha!

> CHRIS
> Owww! You scared me.

> MARK
> Pay up chump!

> CHRIS
> Dude, I'm kind of short on cash.

> MARK
> You said that yesterday. Today is pay day. So pay up!

Mark twists Chris' arm.

> CHRIS
> Ow! Okay! Okay! But let me go first.

> MARK
> Are you going to run?

Mark twists his arm again.

> CHRIS
> OW!! No!!

> MARK
> Promise?

> CHRIS
> Yeah!

Mark lets go. Chris immediately runs. Mark jumps and catches him before he gets very far. Chris falls and Mark sits on him.

> CHRIS (cont'd)
> OW!!!

MARK
I want my money!

CHRIS
I don't have it!

MARK
Then you shouldn't have borrowed it!

CHRIS
I'll pay you back tomorrow. I promise.

MARK
You said that yesterday.

CHRIS
I thought my Mom got paid yesterday. But it's today. She said I could get my allowance when she gets home from work.

Mark grabs Chris' wallet from his pocket.

MARK
Oh, what do we have here?

CHRIS
Give that back!

Chris pushes Mark off of him. They both jump up. Mark has the wallet.

MARK
(Finding money) Looks like you're stoked for cash.

CHRIS
That's to rent a tux for the prom.

MARK
(Putting the money in his pocket) Not anymore.

CHRIS
Help!!!

MARK
Shut-up man.

CHRIS
HELP, I'M BEING ROBBED!!!

Mark tries to grabs him but Chris moves out of the way.

MARK
Shut up!

CHRIS
Give me back my money or I'm going to scream louder.

MARK
No.

CHRIS
HELP!!!

MARK
Okay. Okay. (Handing him the money) Here. Take your stupid money. But you're going to pay me tomorrow or I'm going to smash your face in. You got that?

CHRIS
I got it.

Chris runs off.

MARK
How does that loser get a date to the prom? I'm better looking than him.

Quitting School

INT. BEN'S ROOM

Ben and his dad, Rick, are in the middle of a fight.

> RICK
> You're not quitting school!

> BEN
> I've already made up my mind.

> RICK
> Well, then unmake it. As long as you live in this house,
> under my roof, you young man will go to school!

> BEN
> Then I'll move out!

Ben grabs his gym bag and starts throwing his clothes in it.

> RICK
> You'll be back as soon as it gets dark.

> BEN
> You'll see.

> RICK
> No, you'll see. You'll see what it's like to live on the street.
> To beg for food and money. To always be freezing cold.
> And scared. You'll see how good you have it here.

> BEN
> Yeah, real good. You're always yelling at me.

> RICK
> I yell because I care about you.

> BEN
> Yeah right.

Rick grabs his son.

RICK
I do. I care about you more than you'll ever know. Son, I
didn't finish school and look how my life turned out. This
place is run down. Our car—I barely make enough for us
to live on. But Ben, you're smart. You could make something of yourself son. I believe in you.

                    BEN
But—

                    RICK
But what?

                    BEN
School is hard.

                    RICK
You think <u>life </u>is any easier?

                    BEN
Forget it. You won't understand.

                    RICK
Explain it to me then. Why do you want to quit school?

Ben opens his school backpack, pulls out a piece of paper
and hands it to his dad.

                    RICK (cont'd)
What's this?

                    BEN
My SAT's. Look at my score.

                    RICK
Six hundred! Wow!

                    BEN
Dad, six hundred is terrible.

                    RICK
Oh.

                    BEN
I'm wasting my time in school.

                    RICK
You're right, you should quit.

                    BEN
What?

RICK
You should quit. You took this test and it proves you're stupid. So quit.

BEN
I'm not stupid!

RICK
Really? Then take the test again. Prove it.

BEN
But it's a hard test.

RICK
Then work harder. If you want to run a marathon, you have to train.

BEN
You're right! I'm not a quitter. I'll take it again. But don't think <u>you're</u> so smart. That reverse psychology stuff doesn't work on me.

RICK
(Laughs) Of course not. You're not that stupid.

Late Night Disaster

INT. SUE BEA'S HOUSE

Lights are out. Then we hear somebody knocking on the door. Sue Bea enters the room, turns on the light and looks through the peep hole. She then opens the door.

> **SUE BEA**
> Chuck, what are you doing here?

> **CHUCK**
> I'm glad you're home.

> **SUE BEA**
> It's three o'clock in the morning, where else would I be?

> **CHUCK**
> It's that late? I'm sorry. Are your parents home?

> **SUE BEA**
> No, they went to visit my sister at college. If they find out I had a boy in the house, they'll kill me.

> **CHUCK**
> That's okay, I'm not staying. I just came by to tell you I'm leaving town.

> **SUE BEA**
> Leaving?

> **CHUCK**
> My dad threw me out of the house.

> **SUE BEA**
> Again?

> **CHUCK**
> Yeah.

> **SUE BEA**
> Was he drinking?

> **CHUCK**
> Worse.

> **SUE BEA**
> But isn't he on probation?

> **CHUCK**
> I already called his parole officer. He heard me talking to him. And that's when he kicked me out.

SUE BEA
Where are you going?

CHUCK
I don't know. I have a cousin in Detroit.

SUE BEA
Michigan? That's a two day drive.

CHUCK
I'll hitchhike probably.

SUE BEA
That's crazy.

CHUCK
(Sits on the coach) Well, I can't walk.

A beat. Chuck starts to cry. Sue Bea walks over and puts her arm around him.

SUE BEA
I'm sorry.

CHUCK
If my mom was alive...

SUE BEA
...yeah. I know.

CHUCK
He tries to stay off of it.

SUE BEA
He's sick.

CHUCK
He's mean.

SUE BEA
That, too.

Chuck looks at Sue Bea. Then he leans in to kiss her. At the last second she pulls back.

CHUCK
I'm sorry.

SUE BEA
I can't. You shouldn't be here.

CHUCK
(Getting up) I'm sorry. I'll leave.

SUE BEA
Wait. Where are you going to sleep?

CHUCK
...I don't know.

A beat.

SUE BEA
You can sleep here.

CHUCK
Really?

SUE BEA
...on the coach.

CHUCK
What about your parents?

SUE BEA
I'll just tell them. They always taught me to help out people in need.

CHUCK
(Laughs) That's me, all right.

SUE BEA
Well, good night.

Sue Bea starts walking up stairs.

CHUCK
Sue Bea. I didn't mean to be weird. I just...

SUE BEA
Yeah, I know.

CHUCK
Okay. Good night.

SUE BEA
Good night. Don't worry. In the morning we'll think of something.

CHUCK
Thanks.

Sue Bea walks up the stairs.

Lying

EXT. A STREET

Leanna and Stephanie are walking home.

                    LEANNA
I'm not lying for you.

                    STEPHANIE
Come on.

                    LEANNA
NO!

                    STEPHANIE
Okay, forget it.

                    LEANNA
Good.

                    STEPHANIE
Leanna!

                    LEANNA
NO!

                    STEPHANIE
But Kevin's already got the tickets.

                    LEANNA
Too bad.

                    STEPHANIE
Look, you don't have to really lie. I'll just tell my Mom I'm
staying over with you. And then Kevin and I'll go to the
concert.

                    LEANNA
And what happens if your mother calls over to my house?

                    STEPHANIE
Say I'm in the bathroom and I can't come to the phone.

                    LEANNA
Are you insane?

                    STEPHANIE
Hey, she knows how bad your mother's cooking is.

LEANNA
I'm not lying for you!

STEPHANIE
Okay, forget it.

LEANNA
I already have.

Stephanie starts to leave then turns around.

STEPHANIE
Is your mom home now?

LEANNA
Probably. Why?

STEPHANIE
'Cause I wanted to call and tell her I've been giving you my algebra homework for the last couple of months.

LEANNA
You wouldn't.

STEPHANIE
I would. She'd make you tell Mrs. Martin you've been cheating.

LEANNA
Look, you're not blackmailing me. Call her. She's home.

STEPHANIE
Leanna! Come on! You know how long I've liked Kevin. And now he finally asks me out.

LEANNA
What if something happens to you?

STEPHANIE
Give me a break.

LEANNA
Say you get to the concert and Kevin dumps you. How are you going to get back home?

STEPHANIE
He's not going to dump me.

LEANNA
What happens if he has a wreak or something on the way back from the concert?

STEPHANIE
Leanna, that's not going to happen.

LEANNA
But if it does, it would be my fault for helping you out.

STEPHANIE
You're just jealous 'cause I have a date and you don't.

LEANNA
I can't believe you said that.

STEPHANIE
It's true.

LEANNA
You're such a...

STEPHANIE
What?

LEANNA
You know what.

STEPHANIE
Look, I'm going to tell my mom that I'm over at your house.
If she calls, tell her whatever. I'll be at the concert by then.

LEANNA
What's wrong with you? You've changed.

STEPHANIE
And your problem is you haven't changed enough.

The Dress

INT. LARI'S ROOM

Lari and her mom, Mary Beth, are in the middle of an argument. Mary Beth is holding an evening dress.

>   MARY BETH
> You are going!
>
>   LARI
> I'm not!
>
>   MARY BETH
> Young lady, you are going to that dance if I have to drag you there myself.
>
>   LARI
> I'd like to see you try.
>
>   MARY BETH
> Don't you dare speak to me that way.
>
>   LARI
> Then stop calling me young lady. I'm a woman.
>
>   MARY BETH
> (Aggravated) Please.
>
>   LARI
> You were married when you were my age.
>
>   MARY BETH
> I was stupid! Now put on this dress.
>
>   LARI
> You have no respect for me.
>
>   MARY BETH
> Why should I when you act like a child? Now put this on!
>
>   LARI
> I'm not going!
>
>   MARY BETH
> (Throwing the dress on the bed) Then forget it. I paid two hundred dollars for that dress but if—
>
>   LARI
> You did what?

MARY BETH
I wanted you to look nice.

LARI
That's half your pay check. Take it back.

MARY BETH
I can't. It had to be altered.

LARI
Why?

MARY BETH
So it would look good on you.

LARI
You mean so it would cover my fat butt?

MARY BETH
You're not fat.

LARI
Look at me, I'm disgusting. You can't even buy a dress that looks good on me. And you wonder why I don't want to go.

Lari throws herself on the bed and starts to cry. Mary Beth sits down beside her and strokes her hair.

MARY BETH
Darling. You are not fat. You're beautiful. Your biggest problem is you don't know that yet. When I was your age, I didn't know it either. That's why I married the first guy who asked me out. I'm not going to let that happen to you. Now put the dress on. At least let me see how it looks.

LARI
Okay.

Lari exits to put the dress on. Mary Beth sits on the bed.

MARY BETH
I was thinking you might want to wear my earrings.

LARI
(Off stage) Your good ones?

MARY BETH
My mother gave them to me for my first dance. She must have saved for a year. A teacher's salary wasn't as much as it is now.

Lari enters. She looks beautiful.

> MARY BETH (cont'd)
> (Lari takes her breath away) Oh my. Oh my, oh my.

> LARI
> Do I look okay?

> MARY BETH
> You look beautiful. (Handing her the earrings) Put these on.

> LARI
> I don't even have a date.

> MARY BETH
> Neither did Cinderella and remember she got best guy at the ball. Now let me get my car keys.

Mary Beth starts to exit.

> LARI
> Mom.

Mary Beth turns around.

> LARI
> Thanks.

> MARY BETH
> You're welcome.

Mary Beth exits as Lari looks at herself in the mirror.

The Inside Scoop

Interviews with Three
Hollywood Insiders

When you audition for a television show or a film, the first person you meet is the casting director. I was very lucky recently to have interviewed two of the best in Hollywood. Megan McConnell and Janet Gilmore cast some of the hottest shows on the air. They cast *Felicity, The Practice,* and Steven Speilberg's show, *The Others to* mention just a few you may be familiar with. Read my interview with them and hear what casting directors are looking for from teen actors. (My questions are in italics.)

HOW DID YOU GET STARTED IN CASTING?

Janet - Well, I had been working in a talent agency because I wanted to learn the business. I was an assistant to a top agent. But I knew I never wanted to be an agent. And after a while, I realized casting was something that might really interest me. I thought I might do well at it because I liked the idea of working on a project from scratch. Sort of taking that palate and putting those colors up on the board, with actors, so-to-speak. My background was as an actor. I was never a professional, but I had done theatre all my life: as a kid, in high school, in college. I've always had a real fondness and respect for the actor. So casting just seemed like the natural way to go.

Megan - I've been casting thirteen years come January, 2000. I was in production for a year and a half and then decided casting might be an area that a lot of my talents might come together. So I started out with Lynn Stalmaster in the beginning as a receptionist. Then I worked my way up from there.

I KNOW YOU CAST SOME GREAT SHOWS INCLUDING THE EMMY AWARD WINNING "THE PRACTICE", BUT SINCE THIS IS BOOK FOR TEENS, LET'S TALK ABOUT "FELICITY". I KNOW A LOT OF TEENAGERS LOVE YOUR SHOW. WHAT KIND OF ACTORS DO YOU LOOK FOR ON "FELICITY"?

Janet - We look for people who look real. Who don't look like they are "acting" or "performing". On top of that, we try to cast sort of off-beat actors. The writing is very good on *Felicity*. So we ask people to read very real but to also bring a little humor to it.

Megan - Even though it's a one-hour drama, *Felicity* also has a lot of humor in it. The characters are a little eccentric and quirky.

WHAT SHOULD ACTORS EXPECT WHEN THEY COME AUDITION FOR YOU?

Janet - Well, they should have received their "sides" before they come to see us. And they should be ready to read for us for the part or role that we have called them in on. And hopefully, they will have watched the show a couple of times so they have a feeling for the tone of the show. Then when we meet them, the first thing we want them to do is read. We want to see their talent. And if they are very close to what we are looking for, if they are right for the part, but they need an adjustment, we will give them a little direction. And sometimes we don't because they might be absolutely wrong for the part. But it's always good to come read for us because they could be perfect for a part we need next week.

SO LET'S SAY THEY ARE PERFECT FOR THE PART AND YOU GIVE THEM A CALLBACK TO MEET THE PRODUCERS. WHAT HAPPENS ON A CALLBACK?

Janet - Well, we pretty much articulate with some of these young actors that don't have very much experience what they did that was right for the part. And then we tell the not to change a thing. DO NOT GO HOME AND WORK ON IT!

Megan - Then we tell them there might be a bunch of producers in the room. And not to change it, to make it bigger, because there are more people watching.

Janet - And the director and producer will watch them. And sometimes, the director will give them a little direction. And sometimes they won't. And that is a callback.

DO YOU ALWAYS FIND THE ACTORS YOU NEED THROUGH AGENTS?

Megan - No! Agents send us a majority of the people we meet. But sometimes, we get a postcard. And we see a face and that person may not even have an agent, and we call the actor in. Sometimes, we might see an

actor on television and want to use them for our show. But postcards are a great way for us to see new faces.

Janet - We also have really wonderful associates working for us that go to a lot of showcases and plays. And they help us meet new people.

WHAT ADVICE DO YOU HAVE FOR YOUNG ACTORS?

Megan - Study!

Janet - Study! Do a lot of theatre.

Megan - Audition for as many things as you can and do your homework. Really know the part you are auditioning for.

Janet - You would not believe how many young actors come in to meet us. And they think they are so ready. But then we discover that they've only worked on half of the part.

Megan - Always check your sides to make sure you got all of the parts.

Janet - Be really prepared.

Here is an interview with Rob DesHotel, a very talented television writer. He has written for Nickelodeon's *The Adventures of Pete & Pete*, USA's *Duckman* and the first two seasons of *Buffy the Vampire Slayer*. He currently writes for *That '70s Show*. (My questions are in italics, his answers follow.)

HOW DID YOU GET STARTED WRITING FOR TELEVISION? I began as an assistant to the writers on a sitcom, where I learned the ins and outs of writing, the dos and don'ts, how to structure a story, a scene, and a joke. After a few years as an assistant, I knew how to write a script, and that's what I've been doing for the past five years.

HAVE YOU EVER WRITTEN FOR ANIMATION? I have, and it's a welcome change from live-action sometimes, because you can write anything you want and not be confined by any rules. If you want to write a scene that takes place in a saloon on Mars, you can. As long as you give the story some heart, anything goes when you're writing animation.

ONCE YOU GET A JOB/ASSIGNMENT FOR A TELEVISION SHOW, WHAT IS THE FIRST THING YOU DO? Along with my writing partner, I sit down and figure out what story I want to tell. We talk about the themes, the characters. Then, scene by scene, we plot the story out in a room with other writers. Once that's done, we write an outline for the story. We then get feedback on that outline, and then, we're sent off to write the script. The whole process takes anywhere from 4-6 weeks.

YOU'VE WRITTEN FOR TWO GREAT TEEN SHOWS: "BUFFY THE VAMPIRE SLAYER" AND "THE '70s SHOW". WHAT'S THE DIFFERENCE BETWEEN WRITING FOR DRAMA AND COMEDY? To me, the only real difference is that in a comedy, you want to make sure the audience laughs, and laughs a lot. I approach stories the same way for comedy and drama. I'm oversimplifying, but a comedy in essence is a drama with jokes.

WHAT ADVICE DO YOU HAVE FOR YOUNG WRITERS STARTING OUT? If you want to write for TV, read some scripts and watch some shows. Each show has its own rhythm and pacing and style, and the trick is to inject your own personality into a show, and still have it sound and feel like that show. The best place to be if you want to write for TV is in a television writers' room as a writer's assistant. You'll work your butt off, but you'll also learn a ton. And of course, keep writing, writing, writing.

Scene Exercises

Here are a few fun exercises to do with the scenes you just read.

1. THE OPPOSITE

Many young actors read the script and immediately decide how to play the scene. For example, if the character says she's a ballerina, then the actress will stand on her toes. For an acting exercise, *play the opposite*. Suppose that one of the characters is a football player. Why not have him move like a ballerina? Or the ballerina move like a football player. This works especially well in comedy.

2. PICK AN ACTION

Young actors working on scenes often do nothing but say their lines. Both actors look each other in the eye and talk. But in real life, we rarely just stare at each other and talk. Most of us do two things at once. Take a quick look at the scene called *Lying*. The two characters in this scene are in an argument. Even though the scene is short, it will be boring if all the actresses do is stand and yell at each other. Try picking an action to get you moving. Have both performers fishing, or baiting their hooks or casting their fishing lines, or maybe even nabbing a big one. Try all different kinds of actions with each scene. You will be surprised how much better your acting will be.

3. FINISH THE SCENE

You have probably noticed that many of the scenes do not have an ending. Take the scene *A Friend In Need*. Kirk has told Zip that he is going to tell the officials about the gun. What does Zip do? We don't know because this is where the scene stops. Well, try finishing the scene. Maybe Zip gets mad at Kirk. Maybe he runs. Maybe he goes with Kirk to the officials. You don't need to write these various endings on paper. Improvise. Play around with many different endings.

4. IMPROVISE WITH THE CHARACTER'S HISTORY

Let's take the scene *Cave Boy*. Garrison is trying to teach Ugh manners. Why not make up a scene where Garrison discovers Cave Boy? Or maybe a scene where Ugh teaches Garrison how to hunt. The more you improvise with the characters, the more you know about them.

5. GIBBERISH

This is one of my favorite exercises. Gibberish is sound that cannot be understood. Like blahblahblahblah. To the audience, it looks like the actor is speaking a foreign language. Try the scenes using Gibberish. Take the scene *Better Than You*. The actors will still compete against each other by doing pushups, arm wrestling and running, but they will not speak the lines on the page. Instead, they speak gibberish. This is a good exercise for an actor who is acting his lines like he is a robot. Gibberish breaks that pattern and helps the actor find a whole new meaning to the scene.

Try all of these exercises. And remember, have fun with them.

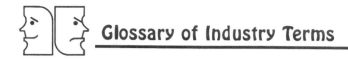

Glossary of Industry Terms

Show business has its own interesting vocabulary. The word *wings*, for example. When someone tells you to go *stand in the wings*, they mean stand on the *side of the stage,* not on the wings of a bird. I asked a number of the kids I coach to tell me their definitions for some of these important theater/film words. Sometimes kids can explain things more clearly than adults.

AD LIB - To make up words not already in the script. If a director tells you to ad lib, what he means is ignore the script and say something your character would say.

AFTRA - Stands for the "American Federation of Television and Radio Artists". AFTRA is a union for actors.

AGENT - A person who helps you get acting jobs. And then takes 10% of your earnings.

AIR DATE - The date that your commercial shows on TV.

ATMOSPHERE - See "Extra".

AUDITION - The show biz word for "trying out" for a commercial.

BEAT - A moment. If the script says: "A beat," then that means take a small pause before you say your next line.

BLOCKING - Stage Movement. When the director gives you blocking he is telling you where to stand and when to move.

BOOK - When you "book" a commercial that means that you have "won" the audition.

BOOM - A microphone that is held above your head.

BREAK-A-LEG - An actor's way of saying "Good Luck".

CALLBACK - The second audition.

CASTING DIRECTOR - The person hired by the producer to find the right actors for the job.

CATTLE CALL - See "Open Call".

CLIENT - The person who has final say on a commercial. If it is a Pepsi commercial then Pepsi is the client.

CUE - Any signal that it is your turn to speak or move. If the director says "pick up your cues", he means that when the other actor stops talking, you must start quicker.

CUE CARD - A piece of poster board with the actor's lines on It.

DIALOGUE - The lines you speak from your script.

DIRECTOR - The person who is in charge of the play or film. He or she instructs the actors, set designers and every other part of the play or film.

EXTRA - A nonspeaking part. An extra appears in the background of the scene. Also called Atmosphere.

FOCUS - Putting all your attention on one thing. If a director yells "focus", he/she means "Listen up".

GESTURE - The way you move your arms and hands.

HAND PROPS - Small things used by the actor. Like a purse or a baseball.

HEADSHOT - An 8" X 10" black and white picture of an actor.

IMPROVISATION - Acting without a script. Making it up as you go along.

LINES - The words you speak from the script. Learning your lines means to memorize the speeches your character has in the script.

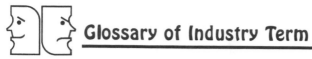

OPEN CALL - An audition where you don't need an appointment. Also called a *Cattle-call* because open calls usually have tons of people.

OSCAR - An annual award given by The Academy of Motion Pictures, Arts and Sciences. There are Oscars awarded for all aspects of film work, including acting, directing and screen-writing.

PRINCIPAL - The main acting role in a commercial.

PULITZER PRIZE - An annual writing award established in 1917. The award is given by the Pulitzer board made up of newspaper editors, writers and professors of major universities.

RESIDUAl - Money paid to an actor for the repeat showing of a commercial or TV show.

SAG - Stands for "Screen Actors Guild." SAG is a union for actors.

SIDES - Part of a script. When you audition, they give you sides to read from.

SLATE - What the casting director says at the beginning of a commercial audition. It means say your name and what agency represents you.

STAND-IN - Extras who "stand in" for the lead actors while the crew focuses lights.

TONY AWARD - An annual award given by the American Theatre Wing. The award was established in 1947. To qualify for a Tony award, the play or musical must have been performed on Broadway. The Tony is awarded for all aspects of theatre work, including acting, directing and set design.

TOP - The beginning. When the director says, "Go from the top", he means start at the beginning.

UPGRADE - Being "upgraded" means when you are hired as an extra and the director gives you a line or makes you a principal.

Bibliography: Sensational Plays
For Teen Actors

If you want to be an actor, you've got to start reading plays. I know what you're thinking, *"Oh no! I hate reading. Plays are boring."* WRONG. If you think plays are boring, it's probably because you've read the wrong plays.

Here's a list of plays you can start with. Practice reading them out loud. Remember, these plays were written to be performed *in front of an audience*. All of these plays have been performed hundreds, thousands and, in the case of Shakespeare, maybe even millions of times.

Your school library should have a copy of most of these plays. If not, they can order them for you. Most city libraries can order books from other libraries in the state. It's called an "inner library loan". When I was in high school, I used to drive the librarians crazy ordering plays.

There are four parts to this bibliography of plays for teen actors. You can't read them overnight or even in a year. Just remember that your understanding of the plays will grow as you grow as an actor. So don't rush. Enjoy!

Part I—A Place To Start

If you've never read a play before, I recommend you start with one of the following. I've grouped them by the playwright's name.

NEIL SIMON
Next to Shakespeare, Neil Simon is the most produced playwright on the planet. At every moment of every day, somewhere on earth a Neil Simon play is being performed.

Brighton Beach Memoirs - My favorite Neil Simon play. I was fortunate enough to play the role of Stanley in this one. And one night a woman laughed so hard she fell out of her chair.

The Odd Couple - A classic comedy about a pair of mismatched roommates. Also a great movie starring Jack Lemmon and Walter Matteau. There is also a female version.

The Good Doctor - This is a series of short plays based on the short stories of Russian playwright Anton Chekhov. Touching and funny.

Fools - Most high school students list this as their favorite Neil Simon comedy. It's about a village where everything is backward.

GEORGE S. KAUFMAN AND MOSS HART
Kaufman and Hart are American theatre's greatest comedy writing team. Here are my two most favorite plays. If you like them, ask your librarian to find others.

Bibliography: Sensational Plays For Teen Actors

You Can't Take It With You - One of the most produced comedies of all time. It's about a family of "kooks" who show the rest of us how to live the good life.

The Man Who Came to Dinner - When a snobby theatre critic is forced to stay with a family from the Midwest, he nearly drives them nuts with his crazy friends.

THORNTON WILDER

Our Town - This drama is one of the most produced plays by high schools. A guaranteed tear-jerker. Winner of the Pulitzer Prize.

The Matchmaker - This comedy was later turned into the Broadway smash musical Hello Dolly.

WILLIAM INGE

Inge wrote amazing plays about the Midwest. He is best known for his dramas. Did you know the best dramas usually have a little humor in them? Look for the humor when reading them. Most young actors make the mistake of playing drama "too heavy". Always look for the lighter moments. It will make the dramatic moments that much more dramatic.

Picnic - Winner of the Pulitzer Prize. Very powerful drama about two men fighting over a beautiful woman. Also a fantastic film starring William Holden, Kim Novak and Rosalind Russell.

Bus Stop - Guess where this play takes place? If you guessed a bus stop, pat yourself on the back. It's always a big hit for community theatres. Unlike most of Inge's plays, he called this one a comedy. Marilyn Monroe stars in the film.

AMERICAN CLASSICS

Here are some of the most successful American plays the theatre has ever produced. Many of them are also wonderful films. Try reading the play first and then watch the film. You will be surprised how different they are. Often characters/dialogue that work well on stage, don't work at all in the movies. And vice versa.

Arsenic and Old Lace - Joseph Kesselring: Hilarious play about two old ladies who try to poison lonely men. The film that stars Cary Grant is equally funny.

Dark of the Moon - Howard Richardson & William Berney: Just about every community theatre has produced this fantasy drama. Audiences love the romance of Barbara Allen and the witch boy John.

Diary of Anne Frank - There are two plays about the young heroine Anne Frank. Frances Goodrich and Albert Hackett wrote the 1950's version. The new version was written by playwright Wendy Kesselman and starred Natalie Portman (The Phantom Menace) on Broadway.

Harvey - Mary Chase: A wonderful comedy about a man that talks to an invisible rabbit.

Member of the Wedding - Carson McCullers: A poignant story of a young girl who is forced to grow up when her older brother gets married.

The Miracle Worker - William Gibson: A play about the early years of Helen Keller. There are many great scenes for young girls.

A Raisin in the Sun - Lorraine Hansberry: One of Broadway's first hit plays about a black family. Also an excellent film starring Sidney Poitier.

Spoon River Anthology - adapted by Charles Aidman and Naomi Hirshhorn from Edgar Lee Masters. A series of monologues set in a graveyard. Did I mention that all the characters are dead?

The Prime of Miss Jean Brodie - Jay Preston Allen: About an unconventional teacher in Scotland. I know many young actresses who love this play. The film stars Maggie Smith in an Oscar winning performance.

The Women - Clare Boothe: A hilarious comedy about a group of women who compete with each other. Check out the film starring Joan Crawford and Rosalind Russell.

AGATHA CHRISTIE

Ms. Christie is best known as a mystery novelist. But she has also written a number of plays. Most of the characters are British. So when you read aloud use a British accent. Cheerio.

The Mousetrap - This was the first play I saw when I was a kid. It is also one of the longest running plays in British history. If you like mysteries, check this one out.

Ten Little Indians - Based on Ms. Christie's novel *And Then There Were None*. The play is about ten people trapped on an isolated island. One by one they are murdered! Bet you can't guess who the murderer is.

JEROME LAWRENCE AND ROBERT E. LEE

This writing team has written a number of terrific plays. Here are my two favorites.

Inherit the Wind - A courtroom drama about the Scopes Monkey trail. If you don't know what that is, then check this one out.

The Night Thoreau Spent in Jail - Just about every college has produced this one. Very inspirational.

Part Two—Challenges

Okay, if you've read a number of the plays above, I'm willing to bet you are starting to love reading plays. And if you are reading them out loud, I know your reading skills are improving. Remember, an actor who can't read clearly will never get a job. So, if you have trouble reading, then keep at it. I promise, you will improve. Now on to more challenging plays.

AMERICAN PLAYWRIGHTS

To many actors, the most important American playwrights are Tennessee Williams, Arthur Miller and Eugene O'Neil. All three are very powerful, dramatic writers. Most of their plays are about very adult subjects. I read some of their plays in high school and I have to admit that a lot of them went over my head. It wasn't until I was older, that I knew what was going on. But there are a couple that I think you may enjoy.

TENNESSEE WILLIAMS

The Glass Menagerie - To me, this is one of the saddest plays I have ever read. Many young actors love this play. Especially the scene between Laura and the Gentleman Caller.

ARTHUR MILLER

The Crucible - Powerful drama about the witch trails in 17th century Salem. Many great roles for young girls.

Death of a Salesman - The tragic story of the last days of salesman Willie Loman. Winner of the Pulitzer Prize. Guys, check out the scene between Willie's sons Biff and Happy.

EUGENE O'NEIL

Ah Wilderness - O'Neil's only comedy. All young actors should check out the role of the awkwardly romantic Richard. It's a magnificent role.

Bibliography: Sensational Plays For Teen Actors

BRITISH PLAYWRIGHTS
Here are my three favorite British playwrights: George Bernard Shaw, Oscar Wilde and Noel Coward. Unlike the American big three, these playwrights wrote many wonderful comedies. If you liked the films Elizabeth and Shakespeare In Love, I think you will enjoy these plays.

GEORGE BERNARD SHAW
Shaw is a wonderful writer. He is excellent at both comedy and drama. Again, when reading out loud, use an English accent.

Pygmalion - A truly great play about an English gentleman who bets he can turn a Cockney flower girl into a lady. Later made into the musical My Fair Lady.

St. Joan - Powerful play about the teenage heroine Joan of Arc. Great scenes for young actresses.

OSCAR WILDE
The Importance of Being Earnest - One of the most-performed comedies in the English language. It's about two gentleman who pretend to be named Earnest in order to woo their young ladies. Great scenes for actors and actresses.

NOEL COWARD
When I first read his works in high school, I didn't think his comedies were at all funny. Then I saw a production of Hay Fever and laughed so hard I was crying. See, unlike a Neil Simon play where everyone walks around saying funny lines, Noel Coward gets huge laughs from people's reactions to the bizarre situations he sets up. To me, the television show Frazier often feels like a Noel Coward play.

Blithe Spirit - A comedy fantasy about a man whose dead wife returns to haunt him and his new wife. Very funny.

Hay Fever - A wickedly funny play about the Bliss family. Each member of the family invites a guest to their country house for the weekend. And then precedes to treat them horribly. A play about bad manners.

MUSICALS
Musicals are often the best plays to see and the hardest to read. Because the book of a musical is only one part of the whole experience, I recommend you read these plays and listen to the cast albums at the same time. Many libraries have copies of these musicals.

Oklahoma - Music by Richard Rogers, book and lyrics by Oscar Hammerstein: The great American musical. The first musical where the dancing furthered the storyline. Check out the movie to see the wonderful choreography by Agnes de Mille.

West Side Story - Music by Leonard Bernstein, lyrics by Stephen Sondheim, book by Arthur Laurents: My favorite musical. West Side Story is the musical retelling of the Romeo and Juliet story with modern street gangs. Having appeared in this musical, I must tell you that the dancing is a blast. The film version is amazing. It won 10 Academy Awards including Best Picture.

A Chorus Line - Music by Marvin Hamlish, lyrics by Ed Kleban, book by James Kirkwood and Nicholas Dante: The ultimate backstage musical. Great songs. Winner of both the Pulitzer Prize and the Tony for Best Musical. Skip the movie. It bites.

Fiddler on the Roof - Music by Jerry Bock, lyrics by Sheldon Harnick, book by Joseph Stein: Many people consider this the greatest musical of all time. Fiddler is the very moving story of Tevye as he tries to marry off his daughters. An excellent film.

Cats - Music by Andrew Lloyd Webber. Lyrics are based on the poetry of T.S. Elliot: Andrew Lloyd Webber has written many successful musicals but none more so than Cats.

<u>Into the Woods</u> - Music and lyrics by Stephen Sondheim, book by James Lapine: Using fairy tale characters, Lapine and Sondheim show what happens after the fabled characters live "happy ever after".

<u>Grease</u> - One of the longest running musicals Broadway has ever produced. My first job out of college was Kenickie in a production of Grease. This is one of those shows that is fun from beginning to end. The film starring John Travolta and Olivia Newton-John is a blast.

<u>Runaways</u> - Elizabeth Swados: A great musical for young actors. The songs are great. And the script which is a series of monologues about young runaways is tremendous.

<u>Godspell</u> - Music and lyrics by Stephen Schwartz, book by John-Michael Tebelak: A fun musical based on the Gospel of **Matthew**. The movie is not as good as the play.

<u>Annie</u> - Music by Charlie Strouse, lyrics by Martin Charnin, book by Thomas Meehan: A colorful musical based on the comic strip character Little Orphan Annie. Contains the hit songs "Tomorrow" and "It's a Hard Knock Life,"

Part Three—Thespians Love These!

Okay, if you've read all the plays in Part One and Part Two, it means you are hooked on theatre. If you read them aloud, I'm willing to bet your reading skills are fantastic! Want more? Well, okay. Here's a list of some more wonderful plays.

<u>Amadeus</u> - Peter Schaffer

<u>A Thousand Clowns </u>- Herb Gardner

<u>Fences</u> - August Wilson

<u>For Colored Girls Who Have Committed Suicide/</u>
  <u>When the Rainbow is Enuf</u> - Ntozake Shange

<u>Greater Tuna</u> - Jaston Williams, Joe Sears, Ed Howard

<u>Master Harold...and the Boys</u> - Athol Fugard

<u>Mister Roberts </u>- Thomas Heggen, Joshua Logan

<u>On Golden Pond</u> - Earnest Thompson

<u>Rosencranz and Guilderstern Are Dead</u> - Tom Stoppard

<u>Story Theatre</u> - Paul Sills

<u>The Effects of Man in the Moon Marigolds</u> - Paul Zindel

<u>The Elephant Man</u> - Bernard Pomerance

<u>The Grapes of Wrath</u>-Frank Galati
  (Based on the novel by John Steinbeck)

<u>The Illusion</u> - adapted by Tony Kushner from Pierre Corneille

<u>A Man For All Seasons</u> - Robert Bolt

<u>Dogg's Hamlet</u> - Tom Stoppard

<u>Having Our Say</u> - Emily Mann

<u>Lend Me a Tenor</u> - Ken Ludwig

<u>Little Foxes</u> - Lillian Hellman

<u>Lost in Yonkers</u> - Neil Simon

<u>Miss Firecracker Contest</u> - Beth Henley

<u>Noises Off</u> - Michael Frayn

<u>Prelude to a Kiss</u> - Craig Lucas

<u>Sleuth</u> - Anthony Shaffer

<u>The Amen Corner</u> - James Baldwin

<u>The Colored Museum</u> - George Woolfe

<u>The House of Blue Leaves</u> - John Guare

<u>The Kentucky Cycle</u> - Robert Schenkkan

<u>The Sunshine Boys</u> - Neil Simon

<u>The Last Night Of Ballyhoo</u> - Alfred Uhry

Bibliography: Sensational Plays For Teen Actors

Part Four—The Classics

Now we come to the theatre classics. Most of the plays below, actors will first read in college. But if you want a head start, then jump in.

GREEK CLASSICS

Oedipus - Sophocles
Antigone - Sophocles
Medea - Euripides
The Birds -Aristophanes

WILLIAM SHAKESPEARE

A Midsummer Night's Dream
As You Like It
Hamlet
Romeo and Juliet

RESTORATION COMEDIES

The Rivals - Richard Sheridan
The School for Scandal - Richard Sheridan
She Stoops to Conquer - Oliver Goldsmith

MOLIERE

(Note: Moliere is the master of French Comedy.)

School for Wives - Translated by Richard Wilbur
Tartuffe - Translated by Richard Wilbur

ANTON CHEKHOV

Chekhov was a Russian playwright. Here are his three greatest plays. Stark Young, Richard Gilman and Ann Dunnigan are considered the best translators.

The Cherry Orchard
The Three Sisters
The Sea Gull

HENRIK IBSEN

The Doll's House - Translated by R. Farquharson Sharp
Hedda Gabler - Translated by R. Farquharson Sharp

BERTOLT BRECHT

Good Person of Setzuan - Translated by Ralph Manheim
The Caucasian Chalk Circle - Translated by Ralph Manheim

Index

Sensational Scenes for Teens!